POCKET HANDBOOK

INDIANS OF
THE SOUTHWEST

BERTHA P. DUTTON, *Editor*

Authoritative information on:
    Indians of Yesterday and Today
    Indian Arts and Crafts
    Calendar of Indian Ceremonies
    Reading List

SOUTHWESTERN ASSOCIATION ON INDIAN AFFAIRS, INC.

Santa Fe, New Mexico

1965

In
Memory
of
MARGRETTA STEWART DIETRICH
staunch friend
and arduous worker
for the Indian

Eagle Dance Drummers — Tesuque Pueblo

Table of Contents

Front Cover Photograph by Harvey Caplin, courtesy of New Mexico Magazine
Back Cover Photograph by Haddon-Branham, courtesy of New Mexico Magazine

Preface

This HANDBOOK is published by the SOUTHWESTERN ASSO-CIATION ON INDIAN AFFAIRS, INC., Santa Fe, New Mexico, a non-profit organization which has been active in behalf of the Indians of the Southwest since 1922.

The Association's function is to help the Indian people safeguard their rights, preserve their culture and to be secure in their own way of life as long as they desire it. We endeavor to make them more aware of their privileges and obligations as American citizens and to aid them in solving their difficulties and misunderstandings resulting from the inherent conflicts between the American culture and the traditional Indian culture.

We encourage Indian artists and craftsmen in a revival of traditional quality and patterns and stimulate them to new approaches in good contemporary design. The Association sponsors an Annual Indian Market the third Saturday and Sunday in August in Santa Fe when their works are judged and cash prizes awarded.

Through our Educational Fund, the Association gives financial aid to deserving college students. Higher education is the most urgent need of Indian youth in the transition from their traditional pattern of living to full economic and cultural status in American life of today.

We invite our readers to participate in our work by becoming members of our Association. A membership application is enclosed.

Al R. Packard, *President*

The chill of many winters hovers around the shoulders of this old sage of Isleta

Acknowledgement

The Editor and the Board of Directors of the Southwestern Association on Indian Affairs wish to express their sincere appreciation to all those government agencies, pueblos, tribes and individuals who have cooperated in providing us with the materials and statistics with which to make each edition of this HANDBOOK fully up-to-date and authentic.

EACH AUGUST . . . OPENING the

Second Thursday

Afternoon . . .

INTER-TRIBAL INDIAN CEREMONIAL

GALLUP, NEW MEXICO
THE INDIAN CAPITAL

DANCES
THREE EVENINGS AND ONE MATINEE

SPORTS
FOUR MATINEES

PARADES
TWO MORNINGS

EXHIBIT HALL

Through the years the Inter-Tribal Indian Ceremonial has achieved international distinction as the foremost presentation of the very best of Indian ceremonials, lore, crafts and sports in an atmosphere of dignity and authenticity.

The Ceremonial has won acclaim from serious and searching students of the Indian people as the biggest, the oldest, and the best exposition of our native Indian people on a "popular" basis. It has been adopted as their own by a broad cross-section of Indian people.

By its emphasis on Indian crafts in its Annual Exhibit Hall, the Indian Ceremonial has been largely responsible for the ever increasing standards of quality by Indian craftsmen and an ever widening appreciation of the beauty and worth of good Indian craftsmanship and art among the Indian people.

To Help you Know the Indian Better The Ceremonial Offers these Additional Aids:

SO YOU WANT TO BUY A NAVAJO RUG? – How to buy and care for a Navajo rug, illustrated in color. Postpaid 50¢.

A DAY AT THE CEREMONIAL – Ten pictorial highlights of the Ceremonial with title slide and keyed commentary. Postpaid $2.50.

INDIAN BOOK CLUB – List of 1,000 Indian titles and publications that may be ordered direct from the Ceremonial, 25¢.

CEREMONIAL ASSOCIATION

DEPT. NMI   BOX 1029   GALLUP, N. M.

10

Introduction

Four groups of Indians dwell today in the Four Corners area – the only place in the nation where four states have a common boundary point – the states of New Mexico, Arizona, Colorado, and Utah. These Indians are called the *Ute, Apache, Navaho,* and the *Pueblos.* Removed from the Four Corners region are other Indian peoples, including the larger Apache groups, the *Yumans* (Havasupai, Hualapi, and Yavapai) in northwestern Arizona; the *Pimans* (Maricopa, Pima, Papago, and Yaqui) in the south-central part of that state; a few Paiute, just south of the Utah boundary, and some Chemehuevi along the Colorado river – these latter two being *Shoshoneans.*

None of these peoples originated in the Southwest; they came in migrations from Asia by way of the Bering Strait into America, small bands coming from time to time. Though they have lived in this country for centuries and are in a sense inherently part of this land of canyons and mesas, their cultures and habits derive from other backgrounds. They must be considered not only separately, each group apart from the others, but also with regard to their remote Asiatic ancestry.

《⁄⁄⁄》

The Pueblos

In and around Santa Fe and Albuquerque, the Pueblo people are most in evidence. They are called *Pueblo Indians* because the early Spanish explorers found them living in compact, multi-chambered structures, and so designated them by the Spanish word for village, *pueblo,* thus the "village dwellers." The Pueblo Indians of today are the surviving remnants of a people that anciently occupied a great part of the Southwest.

One frequently sees Pueblo men and women at the railroad stations displaying their wares, or in *ramadas** or trading booths along the highways. Perhaps one sees them trudging down the road as, with a

lifted hand or protruded lips, they seek a ride. Or they may be riding. If they are on horseback, they take the softer footing along the fence that bounds the highroad, and one gets unforgettable profiles of dark skins and bright kerchiefs. Sometimes they are crowded into a wagon – whose green and red paint reflects good care, or perhaps an old one that has seen long use and whose dished wheels make remarkable parabolas as they approach. They also travel in motor cars, some rusty and creaking, others bright with the smartness of a new paint job, and others of late model – modern sedan, truck, or pick-up.

Traces of the Pueblo past – scattered fragments of pottery and mounds of earth and rock that mark former villages – are found on every hand. There are great deserted dwel-

* Pronunciation guide for Indian and Spanish words: In general, a is soft as in "father," e is usually as long a in "play," i is as long e in "easy," and o is long as in "hole." The consonant h is silent, and j is pronounced as h in "hay."

South side annex to Catholic church, pueblo of Laguna

lings, too, crumbling into ruin, silent and impressive. One never escapes the consciousness of the centuries that these people have lived a vivid and constructive life upon this land.

The Pueblo Indians do not constitute a tribe. Each village functions as an entity, each a group of farming, house-building people, alike in some characteristics and dissimilar in others. The people of Taos, Picurís, Sandía, and Isleta speak dialects of the *Tiwa* language. Sandía and Isleta Indians can readily converse with one another, as can those of Taos and Picurís; and the people of Sandía and Isleta can understand the dialects of Taos and Picurís, but the reverse is not true – Sandía and Isleta are understood by the northern Tiwas with difficulty.

At San Juan, Santa Clara, San Ildefonso, Pojoaque, Nambé, and Tesuque, the *Tewa* language is spoken. Tewa is also spoken at Hano in the Hopi country of northeastern Arizona – where some Pueblo Indians from the Rio Grande valley migrated about 1700. Jemez is the only pueblo in which the *Towa* language is now used. Tiwa, Tewa and Towa are related tongues that derive from a common family, the TANOAN, the parent stock being that known as AZTECO-TANOAN.

The Zuñi language of New Mexico's westernmost pueblo belongs to the ZUÑIAN family, which appears to derive from the PENUTIAN stock. If that be true, ZUÑIAN and TANOAN may be very distantly related.

Keres is spoken with dialectic differences in the other pueblos of New Mexico – in Cochiti, Santo Domingo, and San Felipe along the Rio Grande; Santa Ana and Zia on Jemez creek; and in Laguna and Acoma, about fifty miles west of Albuquerque. Linguists in general feel that the Keresan language is quite distinct from any of the more inclusive families of North America. There is evidence that the Keresans have been in the Southwest "since time immemorial."

The Hopi Indians, other than those of Hano, speak a *Shoshonean* language belonging to the UTO-AZTECAN family of the AZTECO-TANOAN stock. The *Ute* language also belongs to the UTO-AZTECAN family.

A glance at the map (center, pages 80-81) will show that there is no geographical unity among the various linguistic groups. The Tiwa villages of Taos and Picurís, for example, seem far removed from their kindred in Sandía and Isleta. What then unites these people as a whole? The answer is undoubtedly found in their attitude toward religion.

With the Pueblo Indians their religion transcends all else. It is the very core of their existence. All aspects of Pueblo life – the arts, crafts, and industries, social structure, and religion – are inextricably interwoven, thoroughly integrated. From the simple tenet that *man must live in harmony with nature*, the Pueblo Indians developed a rich dramatic art – poetry, legendry, song,

and dance – by means of which religion is given outward expression. They perform sacred rites in their fields, prior to the planting, and conduct appropriate ceremonies throughout the season – prayers for germination and maturation of the crops, and then the giving of thanks for prayers "answered and unanswered," as one old Indian has told it. Their hunts are ceremonially ordered and conducted. Many of the designs on their pottery and other works of art are derived from motifs connected with their ceremonious life. And they build their dwellings and sanctuaries or *kivas*[1] following religious traditions. Through religion all else is given significance. There can be no understanding of Pueblo life apart from its religious beliefs and practices.

Basically, each of the Pueblo communities is a closely united and highly systematized organization. Certain similar patterns of society may be observed among the pueblos, yet great differences exist in regard to emphasis upon various organizations.

Let it then be kept in mind that the Pueblos are broadly alike, yet distinct. The people mingle, but hold apart. They do not favor marriage outside one's own village; it may not be absolutely forbidden, but it is often made difficult. The ritual dances are similar, but there are variations that are closely observed; they are important. Physical differences exist. Taos, for example, which was the buffer pueblo to the north, into the nineteenth century, received the brunt of raids of the

1. KIVA – the Hopi name of the sacred ceremonial, assembly, and lounging chamber.

Pueblo woman grinding corn with a two-hand mano *in a* metate *bin – a practice that derives from archaeologic times*

hunting tribes, and its people exhibit a mixture of blood. Foreign elements show in traditions, societal practices, stature, and costumes.

There are now about 25,200 Pueblo Indians living on nineteen grants in New Mexico. For several years their number has been slowly but consistently growing. For example, the 1965 census shows an increase of 7,820 over the 1953 figures. This represents an annual growth of nearly 3.7 per cent during the 12 years.

The Pueblo Indians made a splendid record for themselves during World War II. Men and women a-like served in many branches of the armed forces, and in all areas of combat. Ten per cent or more of the population of each village answered the call to serve the U. S. A. – more than any national group can claim. And hundreds of Pueblo men and women worked on defense projects. Many have served during the Korean conflict and the following years of tension.

The Hopi Indians are the pueblo dwellers of Arizona. They have a reservation about 631,000 acres in size, which is entirely surrounded by Navaho lands. For the most part their villages are perched on three high, barren mesas located north-westward from Keams Canyon. Within this area a few more than 4,000 Hopi reside. These divisions, with population figures of January 1, 1963 are as follows:

First Mesa

Polacca	579
Sitchumovi	244
Walpi	71
Hano	92
Keams Canyon	132
Ranches	85
Total	1,203

Second Mesa

Sipaulovi	210
Mishongnovi	201
Shungopavi	535
Total	946

Third Mesa

New Oraibi	324
Old Oraibi	148
Bacabi	145
Hotevilla (est.)	500
Total	1,118

It is estimated that the farming settlement of Upper and Lower Moencopi, farthest to the west, has some 750 Hopi dwelling there. There are about 800 living in cities and communities near the reservation, in Gallup, Holbrook, Winslow, Flagstaff, Grand Canyon, and elsewhere. In all, the Hopi number close to 4,800.

The Hopi Indians, for the most part, live on the mesas, although they are gradually moving to the lower elevations and constructing new homes. From east to west the mesas are known as First, Second, and Third Mesa. The agricultural plots are located on the semi-arid valley floors.

The principle sources of income are raising small herds of sheep and cattle, seasonal labor, including firefighting, arts and crafts — basket weaving, pottery, katsina dolls and silversmithing. Among the Hopi are many qualified carpenters, painters, masons, et al., who have but little difficulty in securing employment off-reservation in competition with non-Indians. The average annual income per family is estimated at $1,500.00.

All educational facilities have been up-graded including a dormitory housing 320 boarding school students and six additional elementary classrooms at Keams Canyon, constructed in 1956, and a complete new school at Polacca, constructed in 1956. A new consolidated school at Second Mesa, and new facilities at Hotevilla are occupied for the third year. A new all-purpose room is currently under construction at Oraibi. Formerly, children were educated through the 10th grade; however, the 9th and 10th grades have been abolished and Hopi students go to non-reservation boarding schools and elsewhere for their high school training. A four-year fully accredited high school on the reservation is under consideration, in all probability a public school, if plans are finalized. The Hopi Indians are very much interested in education. Accordingly, attendance is good and drop-outs are few. There are now 85 Hopi students enrolled in schools above the high school level. Many Hopi leave the villages after completing school and make their way in society along with non-Indian groups.

Pueblo woman with bread baked in a conical oven of the type introduced by the Spaniards

SOCIAL ORGANIZATION

Secular and ecclesiastical authority are sharply defined in each pueblo. With the New Mexico groups, the secular organization is in the hands of the *governor*, who is appointed or elected each calendrical year, with the exception of Zuñi, where the office is for two years. Serving with the governor are several assistants and the *principales* – a group of elder statesmen, whose lifelong experience enables them to wisely integrate civil and religious matters. In all of the pueblos there is a hunt chief and a war chief (formerly a war priest, apparently.)

Religious activities are controlled by the *cacique*[2], the spiritual head of a pueblo or of a moiety.

Among the Tewa, the extended family is emphasized – both on the father's and mother's sides. These large family groups often assemble in the home of some leader-member to discuss important matters. Each Tewa pueblo is comprised of two di-

2. CACIQUE – a Haitian word used extensively by early chroniclers to designate the priest-chiefs; it was incorporated into the Spanish language with this significance.

visions, or moieties, membership in which is through the father, though a woman may change her moiety affiliation if she marries a man of the opposite group. Each moiety has a cacique and other officers. During half of the year, the governmental and ceremonial duties of the pueblo are in the hands of the Summer moiety, while the Winter moiety has charge of obligations for the other half-year. Within each moiety there are certain religious societies, dedicated to specific practices; but other societies, also of a religious nature, take members from each of the moieties.

Within the Keres peoples, social organization is somewhat more unified. There is but one cacique, or chief priest, aided by a council made up of the heads of religious societies, all serving for life.

The Tiwa and Jemez people show variations which incorporate certain traits from both the Tewa and Keres patterns. But only among the Tewa is village control divided on the half-year basis.

Religious societies use small kivas or ceremonial rooms for their meetings, and most of the pueblos have one or two big kivas which are used for major affairs, such as saints' day observances and some of the katsina performances, which involve all of the villagers.

The Tribal Council is the governing body of the Hopi Indians. Members must be 25 years of age or over, speak their own language and have lived on the Hopi Reservation two years. Representation is based on village population. After certification by the respective village leaders, the representatives are certified by the out-going council an-

nually on December 1. Council officers who are elected by the council are a Chairman and Vice-Chairman, who must be members of the council. The council appoints a Secretary and Treasurer, who may or may not be members of the council, two interpreters and a Sergeant-at-Arms, who are non-members.

SECRET ORDERS

An important feature of Pueblo social organization is the *Katsina* cult to which all pueblo members belong. (This word is usually given the Hopi pronunciation, *cot - SEE - nah;* it is variously spelled and pronounced in other pueblos.) The Katsinas are the spirit rain-makers. In bygone days, according to Pueblo legendry, the Katsinas used to come to the people when they were sad or lonely and dance for them. They also brought gifts; and they taught the people their arts and crafts and how to hunt. After the people began to grow their own foodstuffs, the Katsinas would come and dance in the fields when rain was needed. Then the rains always came. Finally, the Katsinas and the people had a terrible fight, after which the Katsinas refused to come back again. They did, however, give the people permission to wear masks and costumes representing these spiritual beings and to act as if they were Katsinas. If this was done properly, the Katsinas would come and possess the persons of the masked dancers, and they would receive rain. It is for this reason that the Katsinas perform their so-called masked dances to the present time.

The Katsina masks are very sacred, since they serve as a means of uniting man and spirit being. In some instances masks are privately owned, in others they are communal property; they may be kept in certain households along with other ceremonial paraphernalia.

It has sometimes been stated that the Katsina dances are "horrifying and unclean," but those white men who are intimate with the Indians, and who are allowed in the kivas, say this is definitely untrue. It must also be remembered that values differ from one culture to another. Things which appear innocent to us may be considered extremely vulgar by those of another social group; and things that might seem obscene to us might be inoffensive procedures to the Indians.

The Spaniards did all they could to destroy these Indian rites. In the east, in the Rio Grande valley, where Spanish influence was strong, the masked ceremonies were forced underground, or away from white men's eyes; in the west, where such influence was less successful, the masked dances are performed much as they were in pre-Spanish times, without such intensity of feeling against white people. In the Rio Grande villages, including Laguna and Acoma, it is a rare instance when a white man is allowed to witness a Katsina Dance. At Zuñi there are numerous masked dances that white people are permitted to see; for instance, in the spectacular Shalako – a fertility ceremony – there are masked personators who dance before large audiences of white people, as well as the Indians. And in the Hopi pueblos the restrictions are even less evident.

Among the Rio Grande Pueblos there are two complementary groups known generally by the Keresan names, *Koshari* and *Kurena* (and by more or less equivalent terms in the other villages). Both are concerned with fertility and the growth of crops. These societies do not perform cures. However, the Keres Ko-

Circular kiva at San Ildefonso, with Black Mesa in the background

North plaza dancers at San Ildefonso in front of their rectangular kiva, performing a C o m a n c h e Dance, as adapted from a Plains Indian ceremonial

shari are members of the Flint society, which is associated with the Turquoise kiva, while the Kurena are members of the Cikame society, and function with the Squash kiva. The Flint and Cikame are both medicine societies and a r e concerned with the health of the people. Each of these is concerned with certain ailments that it may best cure; for instance, the Flint society may cure rheumatism and fever, while the Cikame treats for tuberculosis, whooping cough, and other respiratory disturbances. The Flint, Cikame, and other curing societies work together for the good of the pueblo, and they unite their efforts in serious cases. Cures may be conducted at any time of the year. Initiations of the kiva groups are in charge of the Flint and Cikame societies. In addition to their curative functions, some of the religious societies also have important governmental controls. Membership in these societies may be voluntary or by compulsion.

The Koshari and Kurena have individual retreats, after which each has a dance. Members of these societies accompany the masked dancers in rites from which the public is excluded. They also participate in some of the open ceremonies such as the corn dances, where they dance in and out among the formal dancers.

MARIA AND HER SON POPOVI DA

Popovi Da
STUDIO OF INDIAN ARTS AND CRAFTS

JEWELRY   RUGS   POTTERY   BASKETS

San Ildefonso Pueblo   Santa Fe, New Mexico

One of the rectangular kivas at the pueblo of Jemez

The Koshari and Kurena often function as clowns, to the merriment of the Indians and visitors alike. However, their serious duties are far more important.

The Koshari and Kurena that we see are the human representatives of the "real" Koshari and Kurena who have mythical homes in the east. The home of the Koshari is near the sunrise, while that of the Kurena is at a spring just to the south of the sunrise. Long ago, these beings are supposed to have lived with the people, but when they went back to stay in the east, arrangements were made so that ordinary men might represent them, if properly initiated, costumed, and otherwise equipped. When these personators function it is as if the real Koshari and Kurena were present. Thus they serve as mediators between the people of the earth and their ancient spirits. The Koshari are closely connected with the sun.

Differences in costume readily differentiate the Kurena from the Koshari. The bodies of the Koshari are painted with black and white horizontal stripes (or sometimes the bodies are painted grey, and sometimes with spots instead of stripes). There are black rings around the eyes and mouth. The hair is daubed with white clay and is done up with cornhusks into "horns" on either side of the head. An old, dark rag serves as breechclout, looped over a thong around the waist, and from which cow hooves may be suspended. At times there are rags tied about the wrists, knees, and neck. The feet are usually bare. Narrow strips of dried cornhusks are the symbol of the Koshari.

The Kurena paint the body in vertical divisions – the right side orange, the left side white. There are vertical stripes on the face, orange and black alternating. The hair is done up in a single bunch on top of the head. Ragged loincloth and arm and knee decorations are like those of the Koshari. There may be a blue and red necklace made of cornstalk pith beads. Feathers of the desert sparrow serve as symbol of the Kurena. As Pueblo customs break down, these traditional features show certain changes.

Among the Tewa pueblos the old ceremonial groups and moiety organizations are now broken down and former functions are confused. Traditionally, initiation into a moiety took place in the "big kiva." Today, San Ildefonso and Tesuque each have two moiety houses; the former village also has a circular kiva. Houses of the moiety chiefs of Nambe and Santa Clara are used in lieu of separate moiety chambers.

The Tiwa system is somewhat different. At Taos there are six small kiva organizations, grouped into moieties. Picurís has a like number of kiva groups, and Isleta has six divisions which appear comparable. There is one big kiva, or "round house," which is used for some ceremonies which involve an entire pueblo, and for preparation of clowns. The Tiwa, in general, do not personate Katsinas by masked dancers, but the small kiva groups make offerings to these supernaturals.

At Jemez, the only Towa village of the Tanoan family, there are no moiety houses. Society houses occur in the regular house blocks. There are two big, rectangular kivas.

Much of the Jemez ceremonial organization has been borrowed from the Keresans.

With the Keresans, clans and medicine societies are important. The dual big-kiva system is intimately concerned with the Katsina organization. There are no moiety houses. Each kiva group may have a nearby house where its masks are kept and where ceremonial practicing is done. The eastern Keresan pueblos each have two big, circular kivas. Laguna has none. On Acoma's rocky mesa, each of the five Katsina groups has a rectangular chamber in the house block, which serves as a kiva. A sixth chamber is used for large ceremonies, like a big kiva. Zuñi kivas are also rectangular

and built into the house block. There are six kiva groups, which constitute the Katsina organization. Medicine societies are not tied up with the kiva system. Hopi kivas are rectangular and are built apart from the houses. The relationship of Rio Grande kiva and Katsina groups with the medicine societies is reflected in the Hopi organization.

OPEN DANCES

To the newcomer in the Southwest, the promise of Pueblo dances is often a strong lure. The term *dance*, as here used, has little of the meaning of the dances of modern society, or of the esthetic and interpretive dances. The Pueblo people feel themselves to be a part of nature, rather

Hoyesva, designer and artist for the Hopi crafts shop, Oraibi, Arizona; paintings of Hopi dance figures are shown   – photo by Clytice Ross

than "lords of the universe." Each considers it his duty to perform ceremonies to help the seasons follow each other in proper succession, to promote fertility of plants and animals, to encourage rain, and to insure hunting success. All this is voiced in his prayers and dramatized in his dances – rhythm of movement and of color summoned to express in utmost brilliancy the vibrant faith of a people in the deific order of the world and in the way the ancients devised for keeping man in harmony with his universe.

There are numerous Indian dances which white people are permitted to witness. Some are purely social dances, performed for the pleasure of dancing and having a good time. To these, non - Indian visitors are welcome. Many of the dances occur on fixed dates, each year. Some of these are the culminating performances of rites which have been going on for days in a pueblo – purification rites, retreats, prayers, and sacred ceremonies.

It is well to keep in mind that the Pueblo Indian is affable – centuries of communal life have taught him personal restraint – and so the fact that visitors are admitted to certain dances does not necessarily mean that they are desired there. The Indians may not resent the presence of outsiders, but remembering the centuries in which they performed these ceremonies before the white man came, it can hardly be felt that our presence is a welcome addition. That puts us on honor not to abuse our privileges.

Some pueblos allow the presence of cameras – *if these are carried under permit from the governor, and after the payment of a fee.* Other pueblos are deeply opposed to cameras, and permits for their use are never granted. Anyone taking a camera into a pueblo should go at once to the governor and make sure of the existing conditions. Sketching and note-taking are also forbidden unless permission is granted.

Visitors often commit offenses unintentionally – such as getting in the way of dancers, walking across the dance plaza, or standing or sitting in such places as to cut off the view of the pueblo residents, or to crowd them from their own premises. Others are shamefully rude – making unkind comments about the Indians or the ceremonies that they are performing (as if the Indians did not understand English perfectly well), talking loudly, complaining because "nothing is happening," walking into homes where they are not invited, and utterly disregarding the fact that they are witnessing a ceremony which may be as sacred as anything held in a church or synagogue. The Golden Rule should be observed in an Indian pueblo as well as – or even more than – any place else!

Participation in ceremonials is a communal duty and privilege of all the Pueblo people. Individuals are trained to take part in the dances from early childhood. Some of the most colorful and effective dances are performed by children exclusively, as for example, Christmastime and Easter ceremonies at Santo Domingo.

PUEBLO COSTUMES

Every item of the dance costume has its special meaning. The spruce twigs that are carried, and which also adorn the body, symbolize longevity and everlasting life. Gourd

San Geronimo Day Foot Races   by D. E. Brett

MANCHESTER GALLERY

Ledoux Street · Taos, New Mexico

25

A Pueblo matriarch wearing a black woolen manta *over a print dress,
the left shoulder of which is exposed. Around her waist is a red woven
belt; other adornments consist of a modified "squash blossom" and other
silver necklaces. The blanket is of the now favored commercial variety,
probably a Pendleton.*

and shell rattles imitate the swish of summer rain on the growing crops. Feathers and tufts of down or cotton are cloud and sky symbols. Before he can participate in a dance, each performer has to wash his hair as a rite of purification. Both men and women dance with their hair hanging loosely, the beautiful black tresses often falling below the waist. The crests of vari-colored feathers worn on the men's heads are symbolic of the glowing zenith. The women's headdresses — fashioned from thin boards — are called *tablitas*. These are decorated with carved out or painted figures which represent the sky arch, cloud terraces, sun and moon, and other motifs of a sacred nature. Colors have their symbolism, as turquoise of sky, yellow of pollen, green of vegetation, red of life blood, and black of death.

The men wear moccasins ornamented with black and white skunk fur, to repel evil spirits from the feet of the dancers. In the summer ceremonials women's feet are (or should be) bare, and they are scarcely lifted from the earth, this representing the closeness of womankind to Mother Earth, and symbolizing fertility.

Men's kilts and sashes are decorated with sacred symbols in colored embroidery or brocade. The white braided girdles with long, flowing tassels represent falling rain, and are often referred to as "rain sashes." The brocaded sashes show a conventionalization of the Katsina mask, Broad Face. The design is not embroidered but woven in the weft. These sashes are made only by the Hopi Indians (or by students in the Indian schools), although they are traded to other Indian groups, and are used generally in ceremonials.

The men weavers have, to a great extent, lost the significance of many of the textile designs, but this decoration is always the same in design and colors. The zigzags indicate *teeth,* and the central diamonds *eyes.* On each side of the eyes the figures are called "angular marks." In the black bands, the vertical white lines are called "face marks."

From a man's waist, in the center of the back, a fox skin hangs suspended. Often a string of shells is worn over the left shoulder, crossing to the right hip; and there may be several necklaces of shells, silver, or coral and turquiose beads. Above the elbows may be painted arm bands of rawhide; and at the knees, turtle shell rattles (now commonly replaced with clusters of sleigh bells) and hanks of colored yarns.

The women usually wear a one-piece dress called a *manta,* secured at the right shoulder, with the left shoulder bare. Silver pins commonly serve as decoration on the sides of these garments. The waist is encircled by a woven belt of red and green or black. Around the neck are numerous necklaces, and on the hands and arms many rings and bracelets.

These are the principal costume features of the summertime dances, though the same items may be used in varying assemblages in year-round ceremonies. Through them all forms of life are represented: animals, birds, and shells of the sea; vegetation of all kinds; all the elements, and features of the universe.

FIESTAS

Each pueblo has a fixed date for a ceremonial, or *fiesta,* in honor of its patron saint, as introduced by the

One of the rectangular kivas at the pueblo of Zuñi

Spaniards. In pre - Spanish times, the Pueblos had certain set or relatively fixed dates for ritual observances. The priests found it advantageous to select the name of an appropriate saint for such ceremonies, hoping gradually to accomplish a transfer from veneration of an Indian deity to reverence for a Catholic patron. They were in part successful. In one way or another, saints' names were applied to each of the villages, with accompanying fiestas. Now there is a blending of Indian and Christian ceremony.

Mass is held in the morning in the Catholic church of the pueblo, and the Indians in the audience and choir take their parts in the service with apparently the same reverence and fervor that they bring to their own ceremonial. After mass the image of the saint is carried into the plaza, placed under an arbor of boughs (ramada), and the Indian dance goes on in front of this improvised shrine. The Indian cosmogony includes many supernatural beings, and so they seem able to accept the Christian God even while holding to their own faith. Throughout the dancing, Indians may be observed going into the ramada and dropping on their knees before the image of the saint.

CORN DANCES

The so - called corn, or tablita, dances are probably seen most frequently. Corn was for centuries the main staple of the Pueblo Indians. It came to be more than food, taking on a symbolic form. The corn fetish is most sacred. Corn is exchanged as a sign of friendship. The public performance which we see is the culmination of purification rites that take place in the kiva, lasting from one to five days. The corn dances relate to the germination, maturation, and harvesting of the crop and, therefore, are held throughout the summer months. All summer ceremonies are concerned with rain. The corn ceremonies may by very spectacular.

A typical Corn Dance, as that at Santo Domingo, may begin with historical pageantry. First, one sees the Koshari emerging from the Turquoise kiva. These ghostly figures encircle both divisions of the pueblo, thus symbolically throwing the protection of the ancestral spirits around all the people. They will perhaps meet the Kurena who have come forth from the Squash kiva, and an excited conference takes place. Runners are sent out in the cardinal directions. They disappear into the kivas or rooms of nearby houses. The spirited parley continues.

After a time the runner from the east arrives, and the excited throng crowds around him to receive his message. There are animated speeches, accompanied by dramatic gestures. The runner from the west comes in, and the same performance is repeated. These are the runners who, having been sent to the frontiers, have brought messages about the enemies – Apache, Comanche, Navaho – gathered for raids on the Pueblo crops. Then from the north and south, runners arrive with liquids of which all partake — a rite of purification before the warriors set forth to meet the enemy. One then sees a dramatization which may be interpreted as preparation for battle. After its conclusion, the participants file back into the kivas, and the historical portion of the ceremony ends.

Where the two-kiva system prevails, one will observe a great standard, a ceremonial wand, erected on the roof of each kiva. By watching these, it is possible to know when dancing in the plaza is about to begin. Finally, one of the wands is taken down, and elaborately costumed figures, equal numbers of men and women, alternating, come forth from the kiva. The Summer People usually emerge first. They form into two rows and enter the plaza, following a rain priest who carries the great wand. They are accompanied by a drummer and male chorus who provide the rhythm for the dance.

The wand is highly symbolic. At the top of a pole some fifteen feet in length is a bunch of brilliantly colored feathers, traditionally those of the macaw. Just below this cluster are bunches of parrot and woodpecker feathers, tied on with strands of colored beads and ocean shells. Near the top a fox skin is suspended. An embroidered banner – decorated with clouds, rain, and related symbols – is fastened lengthwise along the pole; it is trimmed at intervals with eagle feathers which float out from the edge of the banner, and a cluster of small medicine pouches. This wand represents all life in nature. The rain priest stands along side the dancers and waves the sacred emblem over them throughout the ceremony. During the course of the day, all of the participants are supposed to pass under the wand as an act of purification.

In a complete presentation of a

Zuñi women carrying jars on their heads

Corn Dance, each group dances four times, and, at the end of the day, the two groups join in a final, grand spectacle.

ANIMAL DANCES

During the winter months the most important ceremonies include the animal dances, variously called Buffalo Dance, Deer Dance, Antelope Dance, or Game Animals Dance. These are dramatizations of the supposed relationship between man and the larger game animals which, through the centuries, furnished the chief wintertime food. The dancers are dressed to represent bison (buffalo), deer, antelope, elk, and sometimes mountain sheep. They wear headdresses and horns or antlers which make the likeness to the various animals even more realistic.

In a Buffalo Dance, the leader is dressed as a hunter; and there may be several other hunters. The animal dancers are usually in two lines, with a woman, or two, between them. In December the woman wears a sun symbol on her back, and she is called the Buffalo Mother (or the Buffalo Woman); but in January, she wears a feathered headdress, and is then called the Wild Turkey. The Buffalo Mother is the symbolic mother of the larger animal life of the region. At dawn, she goes out to look for game, and leads the animals to the village. The coming in of these animals from the hills surrounding a pueblo and the pantomime which follows is one of the most spectacular dramas that one is ever likely to see. Small evergreen trees may be planted in the plaza, suggestive of the forest. The participants in the ceremony enter the kiva when all are gathered at the plaza. They come out and dance four times during the forenoon, and four times in the afternoon. The dancers are accompanied by a drummer and a male chorus, the leader of which wears a Plains Indian costume, for it was to the great plains that the Pueblos had to go for the largest of all the game animals, the bison. The final event of the day is the enactment of a hunt. In the end the game is "killed," and the limp bodies are carried from the plaza. The other animal dances are performed along these general lines.

EAGLE DANCE

The Eagle Dance as we see it today is a fragmentary representation of a ceremony which was formerly common to all the pueblos. It is performed in the early spring, and is likely to be repeated throughout the year. The eagle is supposed to have direct intercourse with the sky powers, and is much venerated. It is not uncommon, even now, to see specimens of the Golden or American Eagle kept in captivity in the pueblos, where they are treated with every mark of respect. The Eagle Dance is a dramatization of the relationship believed to exist between the eagle and man and deific powers. Two young men are costumed as eagles, one a male and the other female, and in the course of the dance they imitate almost every movement of these great birds. One sees them in the act of soaring, hovering over the fields, perching on high places, resting on the ground, and going through mating gestures. Although the costume varies from pueblo to pueblo, the basic features are the same.

Each dancer's body is painted realistically; he wears a kilt, usually decorated with an undulating ser-

Eagle dancers at Tesuque

Santa Clara Corn Dance, an original painting by Pablita Velarde, famous Santa Clara artist

pent design. On the head is a close fitting headdress covered with feathers; the eyes are indicated, and at the front is a long beak – in all, a very good representation of an eagle's head; over the shoulders and attached to the arms are great feathered wings; and a feathered tail is attached to the belt in the back. Being such a spectacular display of artistry, this dance is a favorite with the public, and is not infrequently performed at public exhibitions, such as the Inter - tribal Ceremonial at Gallup, the Pow Wow at Flagstaff, the Nizhoni Dance at the University in Albuquerque, and the Fiesta in Santa Fe.

BASKET DANCE

One of the most beautiful and significant of all the seasonal dances of the Pueblos is the Basket Dance, which takes its name from the use of food baskets in the ceremony. The baskets symbolize that which they contain – the food which preserves the life of the people. They contain the seed which is planted in the ground, and which must be fructified in due time; the fruit or grain which the earth yields in response to the efforts of the people; the meal which is produced when the harvest of corn is ground; and, finally, the loaves of bread ready for sustenance of the Pueblo group. The invocations for fertility which occur in the Basket Dance embrace not only the food plant life, but the human race, which must multiply and transmit the gift of life from generation to generation. A complete series of the scenes presented in this ceremonial would constitute an epitome of woman's life, her consecration to childbearing and the sustaining of the life of the pueblo.

MISCELLANEOUS DANCES

In most of the pueblos, Christmas, New Year, and Easter are definite dance dates. Generally the Indians dance on these holidays, and on the three following days. A few other dances occur on fixed dates, as will be seen by the calendar on pages 148 to 152, but the dates of the majority of the ceremonials are optional with the Indians. Among the dances which are commonly performed are the Snowbird, Bow and Arrow, Feather, Butterfly, Turtle, Horse, Crow, Basket, Hoop, Sun, Comanche, Kiowa, Navaho, Dog, Pine, and War and Peace dances.

The Comanche and Kiowa dances were adopted from the Plains Indians. In the Comanche Dance the idea of frightfulness in connection with the Comanches has been intensified by the enormous feathered headdress — which was never a part of the Pueblo costume — as well as by the action of the performance. In the typical War Dance, formerly performed in preparation for battle, the body is painted black. Nothing in Indian costuming is more significant than this painting of the body. When the Indian painted himself from head to foot, it meant war. It was the supreme symbol of anger and deadly intent. Many of the so-called war dances are in reality peace dances, enacted in a religious spirit to celebrate the close of hostilities.

-- N.M. State Tourist Division

A five-story section of the Taos Pueblo, with group of dancers entering the plaza to perform a Kiowa Dance

The Navaho

Of Athabascan stock, the Navaho*, who call themselves *Dinéh* – " the people" – ranged down from the north into the Southwest about A.D. 1500, according to current archaeological evidence. They came in bands, living by hunting and food gathering. Reaching the land of the Pueblos, they took much by plunder. Perhaps this is why many of the Pueblos began to live in fortified towns and on high mesas about that time. The Navaho learned much from the Pueblo Indians: farming, weaving, and certain religious practices (and the Athabascans gave some elements to the Pueblos). The name "Navaho" derives from the Tewa word, *Návahúu,* meaning "cultivated-field arroyo." Spanish chroniclers of the early seventeenth century refer to the Navaho living west of the Rio Grande as "very great farmers." And U. S. Army reports of a hundred years ago frequently mention the Navaho fields and crops.

One often sees Navaho Indians at a Pueblo ceremony, particularly at Jemez and Laguna. They come to trade and barter, to sell blankets and jewelry, and take home agricultural products and other Pueblo items. A few Navaho may be seen on the streets of Albuquerque. Their numbers increase as one goes westward from that city; and they appear in Gallup, Farmington, Flagstaff, and elsewhere in great numbers.

The Navaho tend to be taller than the Pueblo Indians, and most of them are slender. They have long, somewhat raw-boned faces, and are more likely to have mustaches than are the Pueblos. Backs of the heads are flattened by cradleboards on which the infants are carried. A typical Navaho woman might be described as having small hands, arms, and feet, with thin legs; long face, nose, and chin; and thick lips. The slanted, oriental eye is fairly common among women and children. There are particular habits which are characteristic of the Navaho, such as their style of walking and of making gestures.

A few old Navaho men may still wear the costume of earlier days, which is not unlike that of the Pueblos, with calico shirts and trousers. But the common attire for males consists of blue denim pants worn with an ornamental belt; colorful shirts, kerchiefs, and perhaps head bands; large felt hats; and cowboy boots or heavy shoes. The female costume has shown less change through the years. Until recently most women and girls wore garments reflecting the style of the 1860's, when the Navaho were re - clothed during their captivity by the United States government at Fort Sumner, New Mexico. From that time Navaho women have worn long, full skirts of calico or some other bright material and velvet or velveteen blouses. A bright red woven belt is usually worn around the waist. High-topped shoes often complete the costume. In recent years, "bobby sox" have become popular with many of the Navaho women, who wear them with oxfords. Some of the men and women still wear the traditional moccasins of buckskin and cowhide. Both wear Pendleton blankets (which the new-

*Also spelled Navajo (Sp.)

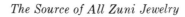

Navaho herding sheep between summer and winter hogans

comer to the Southwest is likely to admire as an *Indian blanket*) about the shoulders, or folded over an arm.

The passing of an era is evidenced as more and more Navaho people abandon their colorful attire for the clothing styles of their non-Indian neighbors. The gay frocks which white designers, in late years, have adapted and popularized from the bedecked blouses and full - skirted garments of the Navaho ladies – the "squaw" or "fiesta" dresses – are now favored by the younger Navaho women who wear them most attractively, frequently with traditional jewelry items.

Silver and turquoise jewelry – rings, bracelets, necklaces, earrings, buttons and pins, hat bands, and even shoe buckles – is the universal badge of distinction among the Navaho. But don't let this display of wealth deceive you. It *may* indicate something of the wearer's own prosperity, but very likely – especially if worn at a ceremonial or public gathering – it represents his borrowings from family and friends. It is often the case that a Navaho removes valuable jewelry from pawn with a trader for use at special functions.

The difference between the Navaho and Pueblo is deeper than clothing, stature, or spoken tongue. The heritage of each is quite disparate. The Pueblo is a house-dweller and horticulturist, first and last; the Navaho, primarily a semi-nomad and herdsman. Property owning among the Navaho is individual. The woman disposes of the rugs she weaves, and of her crops and stock; she spends her money however she chooses. The man does likewise with his silver jewelry, with whatever wages he may earn, and with the in-come from his stock raising or farming (which is now possible in very limited areas). With the Navaho, the mother is the center of the family. The children belong to her and are members of her clan. Because it is taboo for a Navaho man to see his mother-in-law, or to talk with her, a woman and her husband do not, ordinarily, live with the wife's mother, but they erect a *hogan* nearby so that the woman and her children can frequent the maternal abode. Most of the property, crops, and livestock is owned by the woman. The man represents his family in public and at ceremonials.

As non-Indian patterns of life are forced upon the Navaho people, especially in areas peripheral to their reservation or in centers of industrial advancement, breakdown of their customs and values frequently result in irresponsibility, poverty, and insecurity for the womenfolk and children, and general confusion. The younger Indians, naturally, are adjusting more easily, and the better their education the more readily they attune themselves to the complicated situations of modern existence.

When the United States government took over the Navaho territory in 1849, the Navaho were a warring, raiding tribe. After several years, Kit Carson was commissioned to round up these marauders and move them to a reservation in eastern New Mexico. Carson destroyed the Navaho sheep, orchards, and food supply, took their horses, and forced those people not captured to surrender. Thus, in 1863, about 8,000 Navaho were taken to Fort Sumner. Five years later, the Navaho signed a treaty with the United States, and were al-

Navaho woman weaving, while her baby on a cradleboard watches with interest

lowed to return to their old homeland.

The current population figure for the Navaho is estimated to be about 92,000. At the present time they are increasing at a rate greater than 3.0 per cent a year. There are now about 31,650 Navaho living in New Mexico, 57,200 in Arizona, and 3,325 in Utah. Until the present time, they have never gathered in a community that could be called a village. They live, primarily, on a 16,000,000 - acre reservation which lies in northwestern New Mexico, northeastern Arizona, and southeastern Utah. The acreage is not being increased, and much of the land is semi-desert, sandy or rocky, unfit for use. In certain areas, 240 acres are needed for the pasturage of one sheep for a year. There are approximately 68,000 acres of farmland. The acreage under irrigation varies with conditions, as it includes non-engineered projects as well as engineered ones. At present, about 10,213 acres are under irrigation, but the San Juan diversion project now under way should provide over 110,000 acres of additional irrigable land. Some 36,000 acres are dry farmed. Agriculture and livestock incomes are today significantly augmented by natural resources – timber, oil and gas, vanadium-uranium, coal, sand and gravel – and by miscellaneous revenues. The Navaho people are engaged in big business, totaling in the millions, which requires the employment of skilled attorneys, business men, and officials. The per capita income averages about $645.

Not only visitors but residents of New Mexico are often surprised to learn that there are three groups of Navaho Indians who do not live on the large reservation. Because of their remoteness from the agency at Window Rock, Arizona, these groups are administered by the Albuquerque Area office.

The largest of these Navaho bands is the *Ramah* group, which numbers 1,058. Their land lies southeast of Ramah, to the north and south of El Morro National Monument. Next is the *Cañoncito* group, of whom there are 836. Their holdings are about twenty-five miles west of Albuquerque, a few miles north from U. S. Highway 66. The third group is the *Puertocito* Navaho, located thirty-four miles north of Magdalena. There are 779 in this band; they are called "Rock Chewers" in their own tongue, for it is said that when they become angry they chew rocks. The Puertocito (or Alamo) Navaho developed in part from Indian slaves who ran away from their Spanish masters living in Socorro.

Each of these bands lives in accordance with the general patterns of Navaho culture. They are farmers and stock raisers. The women do some weaving. The Ramah Navaho make some baskets.

Also, approximately 15,000 Navaho live in the so-called "Checkerboard area" – part Indian and part non - Indian – that lies east of the Navaho and west of the Jicarilla Apache reservations.

To see the Navaho properly, one must go to their own country – far afield, and often over dirt roads. On the vast reservation, road construction and maintenance were long neglected. During the last decade, improvements have been made, and are continuing. Already, visitors will find extensive changes for the better. There are hundreds of miles of bituminous surfaced highways, and even more graveled roadways. As they are completed, major routes are accepted by the states, which thereafter maintain them.

There are few fixed points where one may find the Navaho. Some may be loitering around the trading posts, buying groceries or clothing, or pawning or selling their jewelry, moccasins, or blankets. Occasionally, one comes upon them by accident, herding their sheep or crowding the animals around a water hole or tank.

Navaho dwellings or hogans (ho-GAHNS) – constructed of logs and mud, or sometimes of stone – will be seen here and there, rarely more than two or three together. In daytime, one is likely to pass by without seeing them, so well do they blend with the natural setting; at nighttime, one is surprised at the number of fires whose flickering light gives evidence of a Navaho dwelling or camp near at hand. Near the hogan or under the shelter of a brush-covered ramada, one or more Navaho women may be seen weaving on the traditional upright loom. Small children will be playing nearby, or perhaps helping card the wool. The older children and the husband are usually away, herding sheep or making an errand to the trading post. The women herd sheep, too.

During World War II, some 3,600 Navaho Indians – about 50 of them being young women – served in the armed forces of the United States, and 15,000 others worked in war plants. Of the men in service, about 10 per cent were killed. The Nava-ho are well represented in various branches of the armed services today.

An increasing number of Navaho now take off - reservation employment. The current placement numbers several thousand annually. This is chiefly seasonal in character, the Navaho working off the reservation for a few months each year, but returning to their homes for the remaining months. In addition, since World War II, an ever-increasing number of Navaho have settled permanently off the reservation in industrial areas. Over 2,100 are living in the Los Angeles and San Francisco areas, in Denver, Chicago, Dallas, and at several other locations. Where the relocated Nava-

-- N.M. State Tourist Division

Navaho sheep and their herders, around a shelter or ramada

ho have sufficient education, hand skills, and acquaintance with non-Indian culture, the resettlement program meets with success.

NAVAHO CEREMONIES

All Navaho rituals are performed with certain aims in mind: restoration of health, securing of food, insuring survival. In the Navaho universe there are two classes of personal forces, human beings and the Holy People — holy in that they are powerful and mysterious. The Navaho believes that his universe functions according to certain rules. If one learns these rules and lives in accordance with them, he will keep safe or be restored to safety. The Holy People have great powers over the people on earth; on the other hand, they may be not only supplicated and propitiated but coerced as well.

The Navaho greatly fear death and everything connected with it. This intense feeling stems from the fear of ghosts — witches of the afterworld. It is believed that the dead may return as ghosts to plague the living. Therefore, any dead person is a potential danger. Ghosts are believed to take the form of human beings, animals, birds, or whirlwinds, spots of fire, etc. They appear only after dark or before the approach of death. Ghosts may not do harm to an individual only, but they foreshadow coming disasters. When a Navaho sees a ghost or dreams of one, it is imperative that the proper ceremonial be performed or the individual will surely die. If successful, all ceremonial cures are believed to kill the witch, in one way or another.

Disease and accidental injury are felt to result from an attack by the Holy People, and may be traced to some transgression on the part of the victim. The cure must be effected by a specific chant and by making sacrificial appeasement to the offended Holy Person, or by engaging the greater power of a higher divinity in removing the witchery and evil influence of an inferior one.

Should a given ceremonial fail to cure the sickness, it merely indicates that the offense has not been properly traced, and the source must be further sought. There may be numerous chants performed until the patient recovers, or dies. Death is considered to be beyond human calculation. When death of a patient becomes certain, the officiating singer (medicine man) withdraws before the inevitable.

CHANTS AND SANDPAINTINGS

In general, every chant has its own particular sandpaintings. These represent the divinities or some event in their lives, as related in Navaho legends. More than five hundred different sandpaintings have been recorded. According to Navaho mythology, originally the drawings were made by the gods themselves, and were stitched onto some kind of fabric. Actually, these should be called *drypaintings,* for vegetable materials and pulverized minerals are sometimes used in place of sand, and the paintings are occasionally made on buckskin. Nowadays the paintings are usually made upon a layer of clean sand. The patterns are handed down through memory from one singer to another. Generally the colors are obtained by crushing stones and charcoal into fine powders, which are sometimes mixed with sand or dirt for easier handling.

Ordinarily, sandpaintings are made inside the hogan where a ceremonial is held. Each chant has certain songs, prayers, and herbal medicines which are held to be peculiarly its own. But, regardless of what painting is being given, the basic procedure is always the same. When the treatment is completed, the patient leaves the hogan, and the painting is destroyed in the same order in which it was made.

Navaho chants may be grouped on the basis of their mythological association, common rituals, and direction against the same or related forces. For instance, the *Holy Way* chants deal with troubles which are thought to come from lightning, thunder, wind, snakes, certain animals, and other Holy People. The *Beauty Way*, one of the chants of this group, will likely be employed if snakes have been offended. If it is lightning or thunder that is to be appeased, a *Shooting Way* chant will be used. Where one has trouble from contact with bears, the *Mountain Top Way* is the proper treatment. For bodily injuries, the *Life Way* chants are given. To cure one of ghost trouble, the *Evil Way* chants are held. Sometimes a Navaho contracts illness from a non-Navaho, and then he needs to have the *Enemy Way* chants performed. The Enemy Way was formerly used in connection with war.

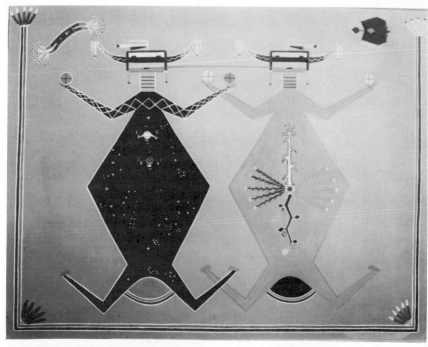

Father Sky and Mother Earth. Blessing painting of the Male Shooting Chant ceremony of Blue Eyes (LUKAI YAZZI).

All Navaho rites have secondary social functions. One of the associated features of the Enemy Way is the so-called *Squaw Dance*. Originally, the intention of this dance was to announce publicly the fact that the girls participating in the ceremony, and who asked the young men to dance with them, had recently attained or still were of the proper age for marriage. The young men came to sing and to look over the girls. And crowds gathered to watch the dancing. Today, Squaw Dances are popular with Indian and non-Indian audiences alike. Groups of Navaho often perform them publicly; and white people frequently participate. Since the man has to give the girl a present before she will release him from dancing, an innocent "victim" may afford the audience much amusement before he "catches on"; and he may also accumulate quite an indebtedness to the girl. The Squaw Dance goes on all night long.

The *Blessing Way* places the Navaho in tune with the Holy People. It is performed in approval of a newly selected headman, for the expectant mother, and for men going away for their country's service or upon their return. Blessing Way songs are sung in the girl's puberty rite and in marriage ceremonies.

Navaho boys and girls are introduced to full participation in ceremonial life by a short initiation rite which is usually held on the next to last night of the *Night Way* chant. This initiation ceremony and the entire Night Way are popularly known as the *Yeibichei* (from the principal figures in the initiation ceremony, who represent *yé'i* divinities). The Night Way is one of the few Navaho chants that has an attending public dance.

NIGHT WAY

The Night Way chant is a nine-day ceremonial, during which the patient is treated. There is singing for nine nights, sandpaintings are made on the last four days, and prayers and other symbolic offerings and rituals are tendered. On the ninth night comes the climax, a drama illustrating an elaborate myth. The Navaho ride in from far and near. They make camp, build their fires, and arrange themselves for the night.

Necessary for the enactment of the Night Way are Talking God (who is also called *Yeibichei,* "Grandfather of the gods"), Born-for-water, and preferably twelve dancers, who represent the male and female deities in equal numbers. There may also be Monster Slayer, Calling God, Black God, Fringed Mouth, and other deity impersonators. With these are the singer and the patient. The dancers impersonating male divinities have their naked trunks, upper extremities, and thighs whitened. Each wears a mask, spruce collar, loincloth of some showy material, dark wool stockings and red woven garters, moccasins, and a concha belt with a fox skin suspended in the rear, ear pendants, bracelets, and many necklaces of shell, turquoise, silver, and coral.

In the right hand, each of these dancers carries a gourd rattle painted white and sometimes decorated with spruce twigs; in the left hand is a spruce twig wand. The casque-shaped mask is painted blue, with

– photo by Laura Gilpin

Painting of Yeibichei *by Harrison Begay, a Navaho artist*

47

a horizontal yellow streak at the bottom crossed by four pairs of perpendicular black lines. A fringe of hair crosses the mask from side to side over the crown of the head. The small eye holes are outlined by red triangles. From the front of the mask a snout projects; at its base is a fringe of fur. Two eagle plumes and a bunch of owl feathers are affixed to the mask.

The dancers who impersonate the female deities are usually small men or youths. Sometimes women take part, and when they do, they are dressed in ordinary female costume, with which they wear the same mask as the men. They carry no rattles, but have spruce wands in each hand. They have no fox skin and wear no blanket; and they dance a different step from that of the men. The body of each of the men is whitened like those of the other male personators. Each wears an ornate kilt or scarf around his hips, concha belt with fox skin hanging from behind, the dark wool stockings and moccasins, ear pendants, necklaces, and bracelets, and a mask with collar of spruce twigs. In each hand, he carries spruce twigs.

These men sing in falsetto. Their masks cover only the face and throat, and the hair flows freely. These masks are nearly square, with the top slightly rounded; there is an "ear" on either side. The masks are painted blue, the ears white; eye margins are black triangles, and a square field of black surrounds the mouth hole. A piece of red cloth usually hangs from the bottom of the mask; it may be embellished with beads, bits of shell, or other articles of adornment. A piece of abalone shell is tied to the center of the top, and turkey, eagle or woodpecker feathers are stuck behind it. Sometimes there is a fringe of short hair at the upper margin of the mask.

The dancers are dressed and painted in the medicine hogan. Then they go into an arbor at the opposite end of the cleared area in front of the hogan, where they get their masks, wands, and rattles. The performance is in two parts. Outside, there is mostly dancing and song; while within the hogan there is chanting but no dancing.

One will become conscious of soft singing, accompanied by the swishing rhythm of rattles, coming from the hogan. After a time the performers enter the dancing area. The singer (medicine man) leads the procession. He is followed by Talking God, then the dancers in single file, and Born-for-water brings up the rear. When they reach the front of the hogan, the singer turns and faces the others, who halt. The patient, warned by a call, comes from the hogan. Then the patient and the singer walk down along the line of dancers, from west to east. As they pass, the singer takes meal from a basket carried by the patient, and sprinkles it on the right arm of each dancer; sometimes the patient also goes through this sprinkling procedure. The patient and singer turn, sunwise, and retrace their steps to the front of the hogan and face the dancers. The latter have taken up the sprinkling movements and continue to make them. Then follows whooping, shaking of rattles, and the dancing and singing get under way.

Born - for - water serves as clown. While the others are dancing, he engages in all sorts of capers, getting in their way, sometimes imitating

Talking God, losing some item of attire and then making a great to-do about it, dancing, and acting as buffoon in general.

Throughout the night, different acts are performed in an orderly and regular manner. The participants take short rest periods. It is said that the most desirable number of repetitions for the dance is forty-eight, when four sets of dancers perform twelve times each. But there are many variations from the standard. After the dancers have finished their last song, the singers inside the hogan chant the four Finishing Hymns. Those who are near the hogan may hear this singing, but few white men are privileged to witness the ceremoney within the medicine lodge. As the last verse is sung, the singer turns an inverted basket drum over toward the west, making movements as though he were releasing winged insects from under the basket and driving them out through the smoke hole in the roof; he blows a breath after the invisible insects as they supposedly depart. While this song is sung, an assistant singer applies meal to the lower jaw of the patient. Finally, there is an act of unraveling the drumstick. While an assistant carries out this procedure, the singer gives final instructions to the patient. Then all are free to depart. The patient must not go to sleep before sunset. He returns to the medicine hogan to sleep, and must do so for four consecutive nights. Certain taboos must be observed and definite rites followed.

MOUNTAIN TOP WAY

The Mountain Top Way – commonly known as the Mountain Chant – is usually held on nine con-

secutive days. The first four days are not of particular interest to the general visitor. On the fifth day, in conjunction with the curative rites, the first sandpainting is made. Other paintings are made on the three succeeding days. On the ninth day, preparation goes forward for the nighttime ceremonies – the making of plumed arrows, wands, trees, etc.

It is the final night that is the big exhibition. A great woodpile is surrounded by a huge corral with an opening toward the east. It is made of evergreen branches. While the corral is being built – just after sunset – the head singer stands at the site of the entryway, singing and shaking a rattle. As night falls, the Navaho spectators enter the sacred inclosure and build small fires near the confining wall. They settle themselves to watch the night's performances.

When the great bonfire is roaring, a warning whistle is heard in the outer darkness. Then a dozen lithe and lean men come bounding into the corral. They wear only breechclouts and moccasins, and their bodies are painted white. They carry feather - tipped wands which they wave to the four directions as they move around the fire. The heat is terrific, but they circle it twice. Then they plunge into the flames, close enough to burn the plumes from the ends of their wands. The next feat is for each to restore the feathers to the wands.

From the first event, this ceremony is frequently called the *Fire Dance*. It is always a startling spectacle. A dozen or so dances – each accompanied by choruses of male singers – may follow, with such acts as arrow swallowing, growing of the yucca plant, feathers dancing in a basket, and many other skillful examples of legerdemain performed. Very elaborate costumes are worn by the participants. The final performance is another fire dance around the renewed fire. Before the dancers enter the corral, one hears strange sounds in the distance – the blowing of horns and shrill calls; they come closer, advancing to the eastern entryway. Then perhaps ten men enter the inclosure. They wear only narrow loincloths and moccasins, and their bodies are covered with white clay, giving them a ghostly appearance.

With exception of the leader, each man carries a long, thick bundle of shredded juniper bark in each hand; and one carries an extra bundle for the leader to use later. The leader carries four small fagots of burning juniper bark. All dance around the great central fire four times, waving their bundles toward the fire. Then they halt at the east side, and the leader advances toward the fire; he lights one of the fagots, shouts loudly and throws it over the east wall of the corral. Then he performs similar acts at the south, west, and north – but before he throws the north brand, he lights the bark bundles of the other dancers.

Then the entire group begins to dance wildly about the roaring fire. They run hither and yon, the breeze fanning the brands into long brilliant streamers of flame which play upon the bodies of the participants. As the bundles burn, glowing fragments drop off, and these are tossed about or thrown upon the other dancers. Every time a brand is applied to the flesh of one of the performers, the trumpeting sound is heard. The juniper bundles are re-lighted from the central fire in case they cease to burn. As a brand finally becomes extinguished, the dancer drops it and runs out of the corral. One by one they all disappear.

The fire dies, dawn comes. Three more openings are broken in the corral wall, and the Indians pick up their blankets and blackened coffee pots, mount horses or pile into wagons or automobiles, and start for home. By the time the sun is well over the horizon, one sees files of horses and wagons drawing crooked lines across the countryside.

The Fire Dance is frequently performed at public functions, such as the Gallup Ceremonial, where it makes a dramatic climax to an evning's program.

Most of the Navaho chants can be held at any time of the year, but the curing ceremonials are restricted to certain months. The Night Way and Mountain Top Way cannot be given until after the first killing frost; they are usually held in November or December. The Enemy Way is generally performed after the completion of spring work and before the harvest and marketing season arrives.

Cost of ceremonials is borne by the patient or by his family. Today, this means $500-$700 for a *Yeibichei,* and $400 - $500 for a Squaw Dance. A *Yeibichei* singer receives $75-$150 in cash, plus $100-$200 worth of goods, and small contributions from people going in to the sandpaintings. For a Squaw Dance, $10-$15 is received for preparations and procedural instructions, plus possible additional "take" from contributions during the ceremony. Those assisting the singer are also paid. Equipment, such as baskets, herbs, deer skins, and the like, must be purchased; and all those who attend the ceremonial must be fed. Therefore, all Navaho ceremonials are expensive undertakings.

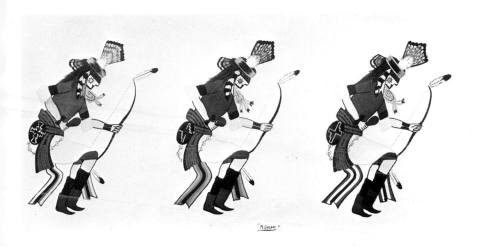

An Apache Gahan *personator of the Mountain Spirits Dance*

The Apache

The Apache, like the Navaho, are of the Athabascan stock. The word *Apache* was originally ethnological with no linguistic connotation. The Spaniards used ''Apache'' from about 1600 on, to include the Navaho and Apache alike, qualifying the term as *Apache de Navaho, Apache de Jicarilla,* etc. Use of the word ''Navaho'' in referring to people distinct from Apaches did not become a practice until about the beginning of the nineteenth century.

The Apache, somewhat nomadic by nature, readily took to the horse upon its introduction by the Spaniards. This increased the scope of their predatory raids. The Jicarilla Apache allied themselves with the Spaniards in their wars against the French in alliance with the Pawnee Indians. They were old friends of the Ute, Tewa, and the people of Taos, but they were bitter enemies of the Comanche and Kiowa Indians.

For two hundred years the Apache laid a bloody trail across the Southwest and far down into Old Mexico – a case of expressing their own wild passions to a certain extent, fighting for their self-preservation in a large part, and protesting against governmental actions of Mexico and the United States. We know the historical Apache as a notable enemy whose hardihood was incredible. He could literally ''live off the land,'' eating roots or crawling animals if necessary, and go naked in zero weather. He had no strongholds, but ranged at will.

The names of the various Apache bands: Jicarilla, Mescalero, White Mountain, Chiricahua, San Carlos, et al., do not necessarily mark linguistic or cultural distinctions. There are, however, many differences that must be noted. In general, it may be said that there are more similarities existing among the western Apache (those living in Arizona) and the Navaho, than among the western Apache and the eastern Apache.

New Mexico is the homeland of two Apache groups: the JICARILLA (from Spanish, *jicarilla,* ''little basket'' – thus the ''basket weavers'') in the northern part of the state, and the MESCALERO (''gatherer'' or ''eater of mescal'' – agave or century plant) in south-central New Mexico. The other Apache reservations of the four-state area are located in Arizona. The Jicarilla Apache are divided into two divisions, the *Hoyero* (also spelled *Ollero*), or ''mountain people,'' and the *Llanero,* or ''plains people.'' The ancient range of the Jicarilla extended from the Chama valley eastward over what is now central and eastern Colorado, into western Oklahoma, and at least as far south as the area of present day Estancia, New Mexico. The Mescalero likewise had a branch that dwelt on the plains. Through these eastern extensions, both the Jicarilla and the Mescalero picked up certain Plains Indian elements – the Jicarilla to a much greater degree than the Mescalero.

After the pacification of the Jicarilla by Kit Carson, in 1868, they were placed, first, on the Mescalero reservation, and then moved just east of the Navaho. In each case, such hard fighting resulted between the Jicarilla and the other Indians that they had to be moved away. The north half of the Jicarilla reservation was established in 1887; the south half, in 1908. In all, there are 742,-303 acres, with elevations ranging from 6,400 feet to 8,200. The agency is located at Dulce. To the northeast of Alamogordo, New Mexico, the Mescalero reservation encompasses 460,177 acres, nestled in a beautiful part of the Sacramento mountains. The Mescalero reservation was established by Executive Order of President U. S. Grant, 27 May, 1872.

The Apache has a splendid physique. Although individuals vary greatly, the people average above medium height. The well formed head rests on a short, muscular neck. The face is broad, with high cheekbones and strong nose. The men have rather sparse beards which they formerly plucked; now they shave.

Most of the Apache men have adopted "western wear" for everyday dress — colorful shirts and denim pants, with cowboy boots, or shoes, and fitting accessories. Many of the Apache women, at one time wore, or still wear, a one-piece dress of Mother Hubbard style, or a loose, hip-length blouse overhanging a full skirt. The latter was never a part of the Jicarilla garb. Now, among each of the Apache groups, the tendency with the young is to wear non-Indian attire. Some of the older women dress their hair in Plains Indian fashion, parted in the middle, with two braids. Most of the men have their hair cut; only occasionally does one see an Apache man with braids over his shoulders. In olden times, Apache girls had their hair arranged around two willow hoops, worn over the ears. Moccasins are rarely worn ex-

cept at ceremonial events. The Jicarilla use natural deerskin for their footgear, which they clean with a whitening substance; they are of a Plains type, with high, legging tops. The moccasins of other Apache peoples are dyed yellow; they have a peculiar up-turned toe and a circular element which serves as protection against cactus spines and other prickly vegetation.

The Apache are traditionally tipi-dwellers. Those who live in the forested mountain dells have built shelters fashioned of brush, which are called *wikiups*. Two types of these structures may be seen, the true dome - shaped wikiup, or a shelter built on a tipi frame. Today, canvas replaces skin tipis. Many of the Apache now live in modern frame structures. A number of years ago, the Mescalero, using tribal funds, built four-room frame cottages for their people. During the past two years, the Jicarilla have built over fifty modern homes on their reservation, and have remodeled an additional twenty homes. They have purchased thirty-five modern trailers. Many of the Arizona Apache have modern homes, while others prefer the old - type dwellings, or use the latter in supplemental capacities.

The Apache have had but few arts, but the women attained high skill in basketry making. Each group developed distinctive weaves and designs. Jicarilla basketry differs from Mescalero, and both are unlike the Western Apache productions. Little basketry is now made by the New Mexico Apaches; somewhat more is being made by their western kinsmen. Some beadwork of high quality is fashioned. It is reported that the Jicarilla are doing more and more of this handicraft. The women find it more remunerative than basketry.

Apache men are good stockmen. The Jicarilla own approximately 20,000 head of sheep, 1,500 cattle, and too many horses. There are some 600 gas wells on their reservation, and over 100 producing oil wells.

The new constitution of the Jicarilla provides that only the surplus from tribal businesses can be distributed on a dividend basis, as in any other corporation. This means the discontinuance of per capita payments. About 200 individuals derive income from tribal employment; some 50 others have positions with the Bureau of Indian Affairs, a few with the U. S. Public Health Service, and others have miscellaneous sources of revenue. Appreciable income is received from lamb and wool sales, wool incentive payments, and from cattle sales. Payments received for old age assistance, social security, and dependent children total well over $100,000 annually. The Jicarilla are making an effort to attract industry to the reservation; $200,000 in tribal funds has been allocated for the training of personnel and construction of facilities to assist firms providing the greatest economic benefit to the Jicarilla people. The tribal council, with chairman, vice chairman, and other members, is well aware of the advantages which they have to offer: raw materials in agriculture and timber products, all-year recreational activities, great power potentials, favorable market locations, etc.

The Mescalero have adjusted

Jicarilla Apache Baskets
-- Museum of New Mexico

- photo by the editor

Tipi and tents in use during an encampment of the Mescalero Apache

themselves to the life of their fellow Americans by becoming farmers, ranchers, loggers, machine operators, nurses, ministers, artists, carpenters, clerks, accountants, policemen, and fire fighters. Highly efficient Indian crews from Mescalero and from certain of the pueblos (particularly Zuñi) have become famous for their successful fighting of forest fires, the country over.

The Mescalero Apache operate several profitable industries, including a tribal store and Summit enterprise, a woodyard and Christmas tree market, the Ruidoso recreation area, soil conservation, and cattle enterprises. Every effort is made to give employment to competent members of the tribe, in all of the Mescalero owned and operated undertak-

ings. All of these business activities bring in tribal revenue which is augmented by fees for fishing permits, hunting, and prospecting on the reservation. The bulk of the income is derived from timber sales, and is deposited with the United States Treasury. Individual moneys are realized from cattle and wages, and a limited amount from small farm assignments.

The Mescalero have a federal charter, which makes of the tribe a federal corporation. They operate under a constitution and by-laws, governed by the Mescalero Tribal Business Committee, which is composed of ten members who are elected by eligible voters of the tribe. One of the committee members is a woman. All positions and operations are supported

57

by the tribe. They have criminal and civil codes and police themselves, as well as administer their self-government.

There are about 3,100 Apache Indians living in New Mexico today. During and after the influenza epidemic of 1918, the Jicarilla population was reduced to 585 in 1920. Since that time there has been a gradual increase until now the people number 1,600, which is the highest figure ever reached by this group on its reservation. During World War II, 36 men and two young women served in the armed services; two of the men were killed. Thus a high percentage of the Jicarilla population took part in the defense of the United States and her allies. At present, eleven Jicarilla boys are in the armed forces. The Mescalero, too, show a steady increase. From 630 in 1915, they now total 1,520. Sixty-three men and five women from the Mescalero reservation served in the war, and a considerable number took part in defense work. The present inhabitants of the Mescalero reservation are Mescalero, Chiricahua, and remnants of the Lipan and other bands.

The Arizona Apache are not as distinctively grouped as are those of New Mexico. In all, there are nearly 10,000 of them. The major Western Apache divisions embrace the Fort Apache, San Carlos, and White Mountain, who number a little over 9,560. These dwell in eastern Arizona, on the San Carlos and Fort Apache reservations, each totaling over 1 1/2 million acres.

On the San Carlos reservation there are two small minority groups, Tonto Apache and Mohave Apache. There are two business concerns which operate stores, the San Carlos and the Bylas Trading Enterprises, respectively. There are likewise some eleven cattle associations among the tribesmen.

The Fort Apache Indians continue to maintain clan ties. There are seven localized groups, ranging in size from the largest, Cibecue (with about 350 families), White River North Fork, Canyon Day, East Fork, Cedar Neck, Carrizo, down to Forestdale (some ten families). They have various organizations, including the Apache Mercantile Company, with a tribal sawmill enterprise, the tribal herd and some ten livestock associations, and the White Mountain Recreation enterprise.

Another 500 Indians dwell near Camp Verde, Arizona, on a 500-acre reservation. Here there are Tonto Apache and Yavapai peoples, who find co-operation difficult. Grouped with these, under the heading of the Colorado River Agency, are the Fort Mohave, Cocopah, Havasupai, and Hualapai Indians. The Havasupai, who number about 250, operate several tribal enterprises concerned with farming, buying, and tourist accommodations. The Hualapai, with population of some 700, have a Trading Company Mercantile enterprise and a cattle association. The reader is referred to the fine work of William H. Kelly, *Indians of the Southwest,* for detailed information on the Indian tribes and Indian administration in Arizona (*see* Suggested Reading List, pages 153-159).

APACHE CEREMONIES

Apache ceremonies have not enjoyed the same publicity as have those of the Navaho, but recent studies have shown that there is not

58

such a wide gulf between Navaho and Apache basic cultures as has been thought. The major Jicarilla cycle of mythology closely parallels the Navaho. Certain Apache ceremonials are given as cures to set things right, or to ward off possible evils.

With the Mescalero Apache, the girls' puberty ceremony is their most important public observance. There are two ceremonies for girls who go through the performance. The first is the construction of a large, brush tipi in which the girls dance to a series of songs, and the taking down of the tipi at the end of the rites. The ceremony is in charge of a shaman or medicine man. The second is the Sun Greeting ceremony, which takes place early in the morning of the first day of the observances, and again early in the morning of the final day. At night, the *Gahan* (Gähan), supernatural beings who live in the mountain caves and beneath the horizon in the cardinal directions, dance around a big bonfire.

For every four dancers there is a shaman whose only work during the ceremony is to dress and decorate the dancers. He performs a ceremony when the dancers are being painted and dressed. The painting of the upper portions of the body is accompanied by song, and the mask and headdress are held toward the cardinal directions before they are worn. The dancers must be painted differently for each of the four nights of the ceremony.

The headdresses are spectacular. They are made of thin strips of wood, arranged in various patterns: crosses, "fans," circles, etc. They are colorfully decorated and further embellished with tin ornaments and downy plumes. The upper, ornamented part of the headdress is secured to a length of small sapling bent to fit around the head. This is covered with black cloth, which falls down over the dancer's head and covers it closely. Tiny eye holes are cut in the front. Above these, shiny buttons or brass paper fasteners are attached, which give the mask a fantastic appearance in the fire light. This singular headgear has led to an incorrect designation of the ceremonial dance. Whereas it is actually the Mountain Spirits Dance, it is commonly spoken of as the "Devil Dance." Since the mountain spirits, or Gahan, are helpful beings who introduced the dance to the Apache as a curing ceremony, one sees how great a misnomer this is. Portions of this dance are often presented at the Gallup Ceremonial and the Flagstaff Pow Wow, where it is received with great enthusiasm.

Also considered as one of the Gahan is the Grey One, a clown who imitates the movement of the other dancers, goes through all sorts of capers, amuses the public in general, and serves as messenger. While the Gahan dance, the shaman, the girls taking part in the ceremony, and the women attending them, carry on rites in the big tipi. On the fourth night, the girls dance all night long. At daybreak they leave the tipi for a rest period, returning when the sun rises.

Finally, the girls take part in a foot race, running to the east around a basket filled with ceremonial paraphernalia and going back to buckskins placed on the ground in front of the tipi. The shaman and his assistants sing four chants, and each time the girls run; each time the basket is placed nearer the buckskins. During the final chant, the girls run

ONE OF GALLUP'S SHOW PLACES

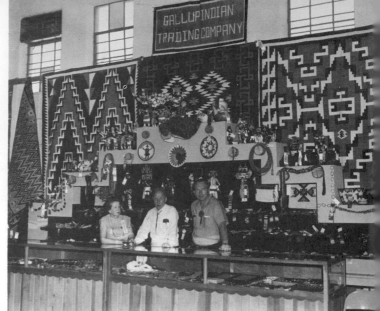

AMERICA'S LARGEST SUPPLY HOUSE FOR INDIAN ARTS AND CRAFTS

- HAND MADE INDIAN JEWELRY
  (Navajo — Hopi — Zuñi)
- INDIAN NOVELTIES
  (Made By American Indians)
- NAVAJO RUGS — SADDLE BLANKETS

S E E ! INDIANS AT WORK

*One of the Most Interesting
Places in the Southwest Country*

GALLUP INDIAN TRADING COMPANY

P. O. BOX 1358   1000 WEST 66 AVENUE   GALLUP, NEW MEXICO

60

Ceremonial tipi during a Mescalero Apache presentation of young ladies of marriageable age

61

to the basket; each takes a feather from it and circles the basket; then they run far to the east. When they return they enter their own tipi. While they are making their runs, the ceremonial tipi is dismantled. Then the gifts are thrown to the spectators, and the ceremony ends. However, the girls must remain near their tipi for four days and nights. They must observe certain taboos. After this period, they go back to everyday life.

The Mescalero hold this ceremony at the beginning of July, the erection of the tipi taking place on the morning of July 1. This is the only instance in which a Mescalero ceremony is conducted on a fixed calendrical date, and derives from the fact that an original governmental order forbade the holding of ceremonies at any other time of the year.

The Jicarilla puberty ceremony is similar to that of the Navaho, being shorter and simpler than the Mescalero observance. It features a girls' race toward the sun at dawn. The Jicarilla ceremony is not tribal, as with the Mescalero, but is held by a girl's family or clan when the young woman is ready for it.

The Jicarilla observe a Bear Dance upon call of a medicine man. It takes this name from a Ute ceremony which has nothing to do with bears. It is performed within a brush corral, like the Navaho Mountain Top Way. Small fires burn around the inside of the inclosure. A medicine tipi is erected at the west end. Instead of drumming on a basket, as do the Navaho, several Jicarilla men rub notched sticks together, resting the end of one rasp on a basket. This seems to be an element derived from the Ute. It produces a resonant, powerful sound which is very effective. While the main ceremony – the most sacred part, with which dry-paintings are made – goes on in the lodge, women select partners and dance with them, outside, somewhat after the manner of the Navaho Squaw Dance, except that there is no payment to be made; one steps out when he tires of dancing. There is a dramatic entrance of a group of masked dancers, accompanied by sacred clowns.

Tourists should not attempt to witness the Bear Dance unless they know the Jicarilla well, and have adequate information regarding situations that may arise.

On July 4, the Jicarilla hold a feast, without attending ceremonies. They have a two-day celebration each year on September 14 and 15, near Horse Lake. This re-enacts the annual reunion of the two divisions of the tribe. On the 15th they perform an imitation of the ceremonial race that is run at Taos during the San Geronimo fiesta. At night a round dance is held. The friendship between the Jicarilla and Taos Indians is so close that each attends the other's feast or fiesta in large numbers; Taos people participate in the Jicarilla race, and a few Apache take some part in the ceremony at Taos.

There are numerous other Apache ceremonies, including dances. In their winter camps, at night they often play gambling games accompanied by amusing songs.

Apache Baskets

Department of Anthropology
Museum of New Mexico

The Ute Indians

There are three groups or "tribes" of Ute Indians today. These are the Southern Ute with agency at Ignacio, Colorado; the Ute Mountain Ute with headquarters at Towaoc, Colorado; and the Northern Ute on the Uintah and Ouray reservation at Fort Duchesne, Utah. A fourth group, known as the Affiliated Ute Citizens of Utah, is composed of mixed-bloods who voted a few years ago to sever relations with the Northern Ute and with the federal government.

The present day Ute are descendents of ten or more bands which formerly ranged over most of Colorado, northern New Mexico, and eastern Utah. There are about 700 of the Southern Ute, 900 of the Ute Mountain group, and 1,300 Northern Ute members.

The Southern Ute reservation totals some 302,000 acres in La Plata and Montezuma counties, Colorado, on the Colorado-New Mexico border. The Ute Mountain reservation embraces about 555,000 acres in Montezuma and La Plata counties, Colorado, and San Juan county, New Mexico. Approximately 200 members of the Ute Mountain group live on individual allotments near Blanding, Utah. Both the Southern Ute and Ute Mountain reservations are administered by the Consolidated Ute Agency, Ignacio, Colorado.

The Ute speak a UTO-AZTECAN tongue of the *Shoshonean* stock.

In 1950, the combined Ute groups won a suit against the federal government and were awarded over $30 million in settlement of land claims dating back to the 1870's. The a-ward was split on a per capita basis, which gave the northerners some $17 million, the Ute Mountain about $7 million, and the Southern Ute, about $6 million. These sums, however, were held by the government until such time as the respective groups could present satisfactory plans for spending their moneys advantageously, and make termination of wardship possible.

The Ute Mountain program for spending its land claims moneys was approved by the federal government in 1953, and the Southern Ute program in 1954. Objectives of both were to improve the social and economic levels of the members, to develop Ute resources to maximum productivity, and to give the Indians increasing responsibility in the conduct of their own governmental affairs.

Both of these groups have made significant progress toward all goals. Nearly all the families now live in modern homes. Health standards have improved. Ute children attend public schools in Ignacio, Cortez, and Blanding. The Ute have made scholarships available to their college students. Well organized police departments have been formed. The Southern Ute law and order code has been revised, and the Ute Mountain code is under revision. Court procedures have been formalized, under the direction of non-Indian judges.

In 1962, the Ute Mountain Indians dedicated a new gymnasium-community building which cost, with equipment, more than $400,000. The Southern Ute for several years

Elizabeth Marsh, a member of the Ute Mountain Ute group at Towaoc, Colorado, shows Dan Neifert, adult education instructor for the Bureau of Indian Affairs, how a Ute basket is made. Basketry once was one of the better-known Ute folkcrafts.

have operated a recreation hall. Both groups have well designed rodeo arenas and race tracks.

The Southern Ute have established their own credit program. Recently, their committees on social service, health, education, and alcoholism prevention were consolidated into a Community Services Department. The Ute Mountain group operates a clinic, for which it employs a supervisory nurse and a social worker. The Southern Ute carry health insurance on all their members.

Considerable sums have been spent in developing reservation range lands; the Ute Mountain Ute have purchased a number of off-reservation ranches. The Bureau of Indian Affairs presently is engaged in rehabilitating and improving the Pine River Indian Irrigation Project on the Southern Ute reservation, a program which will cost nearly $1,-000,000 by time of completion in 1966.

Natural gas was discovered on the Southern Ute reservation in the late 1940's, and oil was found on that of the Ute Mountain in 1956. Both of these groups have enjoyed substantial incomes from oil and gas lease bonuses, rentals, and royalties. The Ute Mountain are regarded as the second wealthiest Indian group in the United States.

Government of the Ute Mountain and Southern Ute functions under respective constitutions adopted under provisions of the Indian Reorganization Act. In each case the governing body is called the tribal council. That of the southern group has six members; the Ute Mountain council has seven.

Traditional arts and crafts have almost disappeared from the Ute culture, although a few women still do bead and leather work for their own pleasure. All three of the Ute aggregates observe the ancient Ute Bear Dance, held each spring. This is a social, rather than a religious event; it is of Ute origin. Each group also holds an annual Sun Dance, in the summer. This is a ceremonial that originated with the Plains Indians.

Linguistically related to the Shoshonean-speaking Ute, is a band of about 100 Paiute Indians who live on the Kaibab reservation of 121,-000 acres, westward from the Hopi-Navaho territories, where Arizona borders Utah. They are governed by a tribal council of six members, with elected councilmen holding office for three years. Income is derived from farming and stock raising and from wage work. Agency headquarters are at Fort Duchesne, Utah, and tribal offices at Moccasin, Arizona.

The Chemehuevi, who now live in Arizona, also speak the Shoshonean language. They were formerly a California desert group, with very simple social structure.

Papago stockowners are beginning to develop fenced pastures for their livestock. Here Papago men, using shovels, post hole diggers, and crow bars, set durable mesquite fence posts prior to stringing barbed wire. The Papago are able to work long hours in the hot desert sun without any difficulty.

The Piman Indians

The Piman peoples have a relatively long history which reaches back into the archaeologic past of southern Arizona. When the early Spaniards encountered the valley dwellers of the Gila and Salt rivers, they asked many questions, to which the Indians are said to have replied, invariably, *pi-nyi-mach* or "I don't know." From this, the Spaniards took to calling them the "Pima." Thus, *Pima,* like the word, *Apache,* has no linguistic significance. The language spoken is a member of the UTO-AZTECAN family; it differs in varying degrees from one group to another.

Pima history was first recorded in 1589 by Fray Marcos de Niza, who introduced Christianity. Father Eusebio Francisco Kino came among them in 1694, bringing livestock, wheat, and other crops which were readily accepted by the Indians. They were a friendly, peaceful, and industrious people. They carried on some trade with other Indians, but this did not comprise an essential part of their economy. By standards of the day, the Pima were better off than neighboring groups, but they were never sufficiently wealthy to evolve a high social organization. Because they did not have a highly organized culture, their indigenous religious ceremonies and rituals rapidly disappeared after contact with the Spanish *conquistadores* and early settlers. The Pima were easily converted to Christianity.

In 1853, the Pima holdings became a part of the United States through the Gadsden Purchase. Six years later, on 28 February, the Gila River reservation was established by Act of Congress. The original acreage of the reservation was 64,000 acres; successive executive orders have increased it to 372,022 acres, which lie just south of Phoenix. Most of the Pima live there; their number is approaching 10,000.

As of yore, the principal resource is farming. Other income is derived from traders' licenses, apiary rents, sand and gravel sales, and land rentals. The Pima have been noted for their skillfully woven baskets and for pottery making. In recent years, their arts and crafts have been dying out. This has resulted largely from pressures of the non - Indian economy, which have forced these and many other Indians to secure other means of livelihood. The Pima have been quick to adopt modern ways. Only a small percentage do not speak and read English. On the reservation there are five day-schools; high school students receive education in surrounding communities. A number go to the Phoenix Indian School; others attend mission schools. The Pima educational level is generally higher than that of many other Indian groups.

The Pima operate under a tribal corporate charter, with governing body made up of seventeen council members, who hold office for three years. All officers, committees, and law enforcement officers are selected by the council.

In June, 1962, several reservation changes were put into effect. Administration is divided between the Gila River Agency, with headquarters at Sacaton, Arizona, and the Salt River Agency, which is located at Scottsdale, Arizona.

A group of Yuman-speaking people, Maricopa Indians who seceded from their parent organization because of a feud, is found dwelling at the junction of the Salt and Gila rivers. They migrated north to the Gila, were granted protection by the Pima, and remained on the Gila River reservation.

In 1874, a small band of another Piman group, the Papago Indians, migrated from the Gu Achi district of the Papago reservation to a location southwest of the Gila River reservation. Their holdings of 21,840 acres, were established by executive order, 28 May 1912, as Ak-Chin reservation.

The Pima Indians administered by the Salt River Agency located on the reservation are organized under a constitution and by-laws, and are governed by a council of seven Pima members. The current population is 1650. The reservation comprises almost 47,000 acres and is located on the western edge of the Phoenix metropolitan area, adjacent to the rapidly growing city of Scottsdale, Arizona. An area of about 15,000 acres is irrigated farm land leased almost entirely to non-Indians. This area, which is on the west, adjacent to urban expansion, is also the center of the Indian community. Part of the reservation is made up of flat desert land which could be irrigated if sufficient water were available. Another portion is rolling desert of spectacular beauty with considerable potential as a recreation area.

The people are well educated compared to some Arizona Indians and nearly all speak English. Urbanization of the surrounding area has robbed them of their traditional

Here, Papago cattlemen engage in a regular, "old-fashioned" roundup, with dyed-in-the-wool cowboys on horses working their cattle. Close by is the ever-popular chuckwagon. Similar scenes could be viewed among the Apache, Navaho, Ute, Pueblo, and other Indian ranchmen, for all brand their cattle as pictured, or otherwise mark and move their livestock.

– Papago Indian Agency

Yucca-ring baskets originated in archaeologic times, and are still in use. The Pueblo Indians favor them for many purposes, especially for carrying, sifting, and washing wheat. Several are shown here, with wheat drying in the sun in front of a home in Jemez.

Artist Pablita Velarde and her paintings at

ENCHANTED MESA

The picture above shows Pablita Velarde, famous Indian artist from Santa Clara Pueblo, during one of her recent exhibits at Enchanted Mesa. Her widely acclaimed works are in the permanent collections of many art museums throughout the country. Pablita's distinctive Earth Paintings are for sale at Enchanted Mesa, as well as her popular new book of tribal legends, "Old Father, the Story Teller".

ENCHANTED MESA
the finest NAVAJO and PUEBLO INDIAN ARTS
by Master Craftsmen of the Southwest

9612 Central Avenue, S. E.

Albuquerque
East Highway 66

New Mexico
299-8280

– all specimens shown are in the collections at the Museum of New Mexico

Upper left and center: Papago cup and basket bowl of coiled technique. Such items are made of beargrass, young ocotillo stems, saguaro ribs, or wheat straw bundles, sewed with mesquite, yucca, and Devil's claw (*Martynia fragrans*). The decoration is in simple geometric patterns.

Upper right and 2nd down on left: Pima baskets of bowl shape, which have foundation bundles of wheat straw bound with willow, cottonwood, or mesquite bark. The coils are small and round. Black, geometric designs are achieved by the use of Devil's claw.

3rd down on left: Navaho baskets are small and medium in size. They are made of sumac, rarely willow. Bundle coiling is the only method used by the Navaho. This results in a soft, pliable basket, which always has a design – usually the one shown. The colors used are brown, red, and a near black which is also dyed. Rims are always finished with false braid, the Navaho being credited with the invention of this method.

Lower left: A large Hopi coiled basket of storage type. The fat, round coils have a foundation of grass; they are sewed with yucca fibers. Hopi baskets are bright of color, commonly on a light background. Sewing colors are dyed with native-made vegetable dyes, as a rule.

Center: Wicker baskets are made by various Pueblo peoples in Arizona and New Mexico. The material used is willow in its natural brownish-red color. A decorative border made up of multi-warp strands is characteristic.

2nd down on right: Jicarilla Apache coiled basketry is made on a 3- or 5-rod foundation of sumac or willow. The coils are sturdy and fat. Designs are fashioned in natural tan with aniline dyes. Rims are almost invariably finished with false braid.

3rd down on right: Mescalero Apache coiled basketry has a 2-rod and bundle, 3-rod and bundle, or wide slat and bundle. The example shown is of the 2-rod type, decorated with the characteristic Mescalero star pattern. Split yucca leaves are used for the sewing material. Different degrees of bleaching produce yellow, green, and white.

Bottom right, above: Twined carrying basket or pannier, decorated with simple banded design in contrasting colors. It has a deer skin covered base and long deer skin fringes, to the ends of which tin tinklers are attached; these produce a pleasant, musical rhythm as the basket is carried by beast or human burden bearer.

Bottom right, below: As the pannier against which it rests, this coiled bowl is of Western Apache type. The Apaches who dwell in east-central Arizona make such baskets with 3 rods of willow or cottonwood; the coils are sewed with splints of either material. The coils are small and hard. Black splints of Devil's claw are used in the designs, which may be life forms or geometric. Fine, even stitches hold the coils together. Frequently the rim is finished off in black.

CERRILLOS, N.M.

On State Road 10 between Santa Fe and Albuquerque
23 miles from Santa Fe – 40 miles from Albuquerque

Since you came all the way out here to see this country, why not get off the main highway and really see it? State Road 10, an old time mining road, now all paved, will take you through some mighty fine scenery, inasmuch as the ores of the earth are usually found in remote places. While scenic beauty wasn't exactly what the old prospectors were looking for, it goes along with the quaint old mining town of Cerrillos, a lively ghost town, not restored, not fancied up, but just as it was with the old store fronts, board walks and old hitching posts. A thirst quenching oasis it was then and is now, and a place to browse around, especially at the . . . .

THE WHAT-NOT SHOP

ANTIQUES   CURIOS   OLD ROCKS

Open 7 days and evenings a week.

PHONE SANTA FE 982-5040

And what not indeed? An eye-popping shop of amazing and delightful clutter – an antique-hound's paradise . . . furniture (even an old square piano), porcelains, brass beds, old carnival glass, wooden butter molds, monkey stoves, sundry books and bits. Rocks for rock hounds. You will want to take a lot of time to turn yourself loose in here. There is no need to hurry in Cerrillos and remember, the lights shine here until 9 o'clock every evening.

damask fabrics were all produced, along with the simpler techniques still practiced.

Weaving in wool began sometime around 1600, after the introduction of sheep into the Southwest by the Spaniards. The Pueblo and Navaho looms are practically identical, and they show no European influence to this day.

By 1706, Navaho weaving was well enough established to attract the attention of a Spanish chronicler. In the following years rapid progress was made in beauty and quality. The oldest known examples of Navaho weaving have come from Massacre Cave, Canyon del Muerto, in Arizona, where a group of Navaho women and children were killed in 1805. The golden age of Navaho weaving came after that date, and by 1850, Navaho women had brought their weaving to its greatest height. From 1863-1868, the Navaho were confined at Fort Sumner. After their return to their home country, changes in weaving took place (1875-1890), resulting from commercial dyes, twisted yarns, and new ideas of design.

After 1890, rugs began to take the place of blankets. Until about 1910 there was a "dark age" in Navaho weaving; quality fell off, and the native designs almost ceased; bordered specimens predominated. Then came a change for the better, due largely to efforts of the traders to raise the standard of Navaho weaving. Art lovers and scientists did their part, too. Again, relatively thin blankets began to appear, with stripes, terraces, and colors of an earlier day. With government help, new soft colors were developed from native plants. Fineness of weaving and quality increased. At the present time, a limited amount of fine Navaho weaving is being produced, but for the most part, the work seems to reflect the death throes of a nearly extinct art — many of the designs are bizarre, the colors gaudy, and the workmanship careless.

All of the family helps with shearing the sheep, but the woman washes, cards, dyes, and spins the wool. She still uses the primitive spindle — a smooth, slender hardwood stick about two feet in length, which is pushed through a thin wooden disc from four to five inches in diameter. The loom consists of two upright poles and two cross bars supporting the warp frame. The weaver works from the bottom up, and manipulates her batten, comb, and yarns with dextrous fingers.

Very little textile weaving is done now by the Pueblo Indians, with exception of belts, head bands, and garters, which are made by men or women, and by girls in the schools. It was the ancient custom for men to weave the shoulder robes and black dresses (*mantas*), sashes, and belts. In most of the pueblos the ordinary clothing worn by the women is purchased from a store or trading post. Ceremonial weaving is largely obtained from the Hopi Indians who still produce traditional garments and accessories. Embroidery, formerly a man's craft, may now be taught to girls in school.

The Navaho women weave some of the red belts that they wear, and these are almost indistinguishable from those woven by the Hopi. The Apache do no weaving other than what the girls may do in school.

Hopi weaver making a ceremonial sash; note second loom set up at his right, where weaving has been carefully covered until work is resumed.

Coochunka, a First Mesa Hopi pottery maker, showing how she produces her "thumb nail" designs.

POTTERY

Pottery making was probably introduced into the Southwest from Mexico. The earliest evidences, found in southern New Mexico and Arizona, date from a few centuries before the Christian era. After considerable time this art spread to the Pueblo Indians.

The making of pottery is woman's work. Throughout the centuries household vessels were created, broken, and thrown out on the refuse heaps. With this simple procedure, history was written – history which the archaeologists can read almost as easily as a book. To reveal the records of the past, the archaeologist cuts a trench through one of the abandoned middens, thus exposing layer upon layer of accumulated debris. In these strata, fragments of pottery – the well known potsherds – withstand the passing of time. Thanks to the fact that the pot makers were conformists, they have provided (and are still supplying) an invaluable archive of their activities. In the various regions, certain forms, types, and styles of decoration, were developed; and from time to time changes in color, shape, quality of paste, occurred. Thus these bits of broken pottery show sequences and modification, and trade from one area to another. They contribute much toward reconstruction of the ancient cultures. If the visitor in the Southwest can learn only a little of what these potsherds mean, if he can place but a few of them in their rightful historical position, it will add much to the enjoyment of his travels through the land.

With astonishingly little effort, one can learn to distinguish the pottery

Pueblo Pottery

Santa Clara

Santa Clara

Santo Domingo
Santa Clara

Zuñi
Zia
San Juan
Zuñi

San Juan

San Juan
Hopi
San Ildefonso

Pueblo Pottery

San Ildefonso
Santa Clara
San Ildefonso

Acoma
Acoma
Acoma

San Ildefonso
Acoma
San Ildefonso

– Museum of New Mexico

SERVING SANTA FE AND LOS ALAMOS

WITH

EVERY MODERN BANKING CONVENIENCE

The
FIRST NATIONAL BANK
of SANTA FE

CHARTERED IN 1870

Member F. D. I. C.

styles of the modern pueblos. Design patterns are traditional and, in the main, each pueblo holds to its own. A Fiesta day spent under the portal of the Palace of the Governors or a few hours at the Museum of New Mexico in Santa Fe, the Arizona State Museum in Tucson, the Museum of Northern Arizona at Flagstaff, or museums in other Southwestern cities, will send the observant traveler away rich in new lore. The sky band, bird, and cloud motifs of Zia; the floral designs and realistic fauna of Cochiti; the strong geometric arrangements of Santo Domingo; the precision and beauty of the Acoma workmanship; and the mask and conventionalized bird symbols of the Hopi, are but a few of the characteristics that will cling in his memory.

By the early part of this century, pottery making in the Rio Grande pueblos had in some instances died out entirely, while other villages were producing mainly utility wares. A few pueblos were making polished red and/or polished black, black-on-cream, or polychrome wares. It is known that polychrome ware was being made at San Ildefonso by 1875; it was the dominant type in the 1890's, and continued until about 1920. The plain black ware, similar to that long produced at Santa Clara, also may have been made at San Ildefonso as early as 1875.

In 1908, while excavating in a cave in the Rito de los Frijoles, archaeologists of the School of American Research uncovered some prepared pottery clay which had never been fashioned into vessels by the prehistoric artisans. The material was given to María and Julian Martinez of San Ildefonso, who made several pieces of pottery from it, decorating the specimens and firing them according to the procedure of that period. The results were very satisfactory. This, and encouragement given María (*Po-vi-ka*) by members of the School of American Research staff, appears to have stimulated her and other Tewa artisans to produce wares of increasing quality and quantity.

During the early 1900's the black-on-red style of the San Ildefonso potters, which appears to have been made as early as the first half of the 19th century, gained some popularity and improved in quality, but the public never responded to it very well. About 1919, experiments were begun at San Ildefonso which resulted in the now popular black burnished and matte ware. Santa Clara began to produce a similar ware about 1930. The first pieces made at both pueblos had the mass dull and the design burnished. Then, with exception of the *Avanyu* or serpent element of San Ildefonso – which is always polished – this combination was sometimes reversed. Today the standardized ware has the mass burnished and the design in matte.

The incised pottery of San Juan represents a revival of an old form of decoration. About 1931, Mrs. Regina Cata began copying the technique employed on an archaeologic ware, known as *Potsuwi'i Incised,* which occurs commonly at ruins on the Pajarito plateau. The deeply carved wares in red and black are of very recent origin in the Tewa pueblos. Tesuque did not adopt this form of embellishment until 1942.

In 1954, the French government presented the much coveted *Palmes Academiques* to two Pueblo pottery-

- N.M. State Tourist Division

*Santana Martinez of San Ildefonso receiving a class award for excellent
pottery displayed at the Inter-tribal Ceremonial at Gallup, New Mexico.
Founded in 1922 by a small group of farsighted civic leaders, the non-
profit Ceremonial Association has been a great factor in the perpetua-
tion and development of indigenous arts and crafts not only in the
Southwest, but elsewhere; Indians from over thirty culture groups, from
coast to coast and from Canada to Mexico, gather for the annual, mid-
August event, where they exhibit the finest of their productions and give
magnificent dance-drama-chant presentations. Thus the Ceremonial en-
courages the Indians to make and display items of the highest quality;
it provides an occasion where non - Indian and Indian join in bringing
the choicest pieces to public attention; and where visitors may increase
their knowledge and appreciation of Indian handicrafts. The editor of
this book, as judge of pottery, has awarded first prize and its emblem-
atic ribbon to Santana. State fairs and those held by certain of the Indian groups, and other annual or periodic celebrations, do their share
in upholding the superior skills of the original Americans; these same
agencies are constantly combatting the commercial innovations which
seek to beguile the public with cheap, machine-made articles which re-
semble the hand-made works of the Indian artisans.*

makers, María Martínez, San Ildefonso, and Severa Tafoya, Santa Clara.

It is to be hoped that the visitor in the Southwest, as well as those who dwell here, will be selective in making their purchases of Indian products. In the markets, trading posts, and pueblo homes, both good works and bad will be found. If one selects good pieces, he himself will be the gainer. And he will also assist the Southwestern Association on Indian Affairs, and others, in their efforts to maintain high standards for Indian-made goods. It will add interest if he informs himself as to the more usual of the classic designs. The conventionalized serpent, the triangular rain bird, the different water symbols – rain at a distance, rain near by, etc.; when he can recognize some of these he will have taken a step back into time, a time when myth was reality.

Commercialization has brought about changes in some of the pueblos. It has resulted in new and smaller forms, often lowered quality and careless execution, and flamboyant use of color in decoration. At Tesuque, for instance, there are several good potters who can produce fine pottery (and they will do so if good ware is appreciated), but most of the present output consists of the cheap, gaudily painted (with show card colors), novelty items that are made expressly for the tourist trade. They cannot even be classed as true Indian ceramics, inasmuch as the decoration is applied *after* the pottery is fired. Jemez, Isleta, and Santo Domingo, lamentably, are also producing similar pseudo-ceramics. However, in defense of the Indian, it should be explained that the idea for this type of product seems to have originated with a white man. The designs are often well done.

Visitors who wish to know more than can be suggested here, will find the exhibits on display at the Museum of New Mexico open to them, without fee. Many of the concerns advertised in this book are glad to give reliable information to travelers. Most Southwestern museums feature displays of pottery.

In examining the collections of Southwestern pottery, it may be of interest to remember that the method of manufacture is as traditional as the form and design. The smoothing stone used by the potter may be centuries old, handed down from mother to daughter, or picked up from an ancient ruin. An Indian woman does not sit down to make a vessel at random. Much preparation is necessary. Clays must be brought in from the hills and made ready. For strengthening the clay, sand temper must be at hand. There are paints to be collected, such as the mineral earths to be obtained for the colored washes and designs, and perhaps *guaco,* or Rocky Mountain bee plant, to be gathered and boiled to produce a black pigment. Paint brushes are fibers of the spiked yucca, or soap weed, leaves chewed off at one end.

There is no use of the potter's wheel. All aboriginal American pottery is strictly hand made. A pancake of paste (the clay mixed with water) is patted into shape for the base of the bowl, and the walls are built up by successive coils of rolled clay, which are afterward smoothed to uniformity by a gourd tool. After a vessel is made it is dried for a while in the air, then the slip is applied and the decoration. Finally the pottery is fired. A convenient dry spot is selected near the home of the potter, and a fire is made on the ground. When a bed of coals is formed, a rude grate is constructed from any items at hand – bits of iron, stones, old bricks, tin cans. Then the pottery is arranged over the grate, upside down. Cakes of dried dung are placed around and over the vessels. The fire is renewed, probably with shredded juniper bark. Small pieces of dung are tucked into the crevices, but space is left for air to circulate.

The black pottery is a highly polished red before it goes into the fire. If it is to remain red, it is fired with an oxidizing flame. If black is desired, the fire is smothered with fine, loose manure, permitting the smudge or carbon to penetrate the porous clay.

Hopi pottery has shown much de-

generation, but good pieces are still produced on First Mesa. In southern Arizona, as among the Maricopa, a paddle-and-anvil method was used, rather than coiling.

The Apache Indians have not made pottery for a number of years. The Navaho continue to make their traditional vessels in some quantity, cylindrical pots with pointed bottoms, which may be arranged easily in the coals of a campfire. From the Pueblos they have learned to make certain Pueblo-like pieces, which are primarily decorated with red on a buff colored background. Tin cans and commercially manufactured utensils are too readily available to make pottery production worth the effort to most of the Navaho of today.

Many fine examples of Indian pottery are for sale by the firms whose advertisements appear in this handbook.

The skillful hands of María, of San Ildefonso, shaping the base of a new pottery vessel in the bottom of an old bowl

JEWELRY

Often we speak of turquoise and silver in the same breath. But turquoise has been cherished by the Southwestern Indians for centuries, while the use of silver came to them through white men. The cult of the turquoise goes into legendary backgrounds. The stone was said to have benign powers; even a bead of it tied in the hair would ward off calamity, and the wearer would be immune to many of life's hazards. The Indians have traveled great distances to obtain turquoise. The hard, deep blue stones have always been the most prized.

Metal work among the Navaho dates from about the middle of the nineteenth century. The first work was done in iron. A few learned metal working from the Spanish-Americans, but it was mainly while detained at Fort Sumner that some of the Navaho men learned the craft. There they were given coils of brass and copper which they fashioned into bracelets and ornaments for ring bits. No silver work was done until after the Navaho returned home from Fort Sumner. From then on the production of silver increased gradually. Their equipment was incredibly crude. One of the early metal workers used a discarded shovel as a melting pot, and his tools were scissors, a hammer, and a file. Bells were hammered from quarters, and American dollars were melted and made into tobacco canteens, bridles, bow guards, etc. Then the United States coins were discarded for the Mexican *peso*, which was richer in silver content and more malleable. The Indians now use slug, sheet, and wire silver.

A wide range of silver articles, in many patterns and for many uses, is now made by the Navaho, but the objects they make primarily for their own gratification as well as that of the tourist are largely items of personal adornment: conchas for belts, buttons, bracelets, finger rings, earrings, nécklaces, hat bands, and so on. The common type of Navaho necklace is made of large, hollow, silver beads separated by flower-shaped pendants, with a crescent-shaped ornament in front. These are generally called "squash blossom" necklaces, from the pendant features. Actually, this is a misnomer, for the blossom element is derived from the Mexican trouser and jacket ornaments fashioned to represent the young fruit of the pomegranate. The pomegranate pattern has been a favorite Spanish design for centuries. The terminal crescent, or *najah*, which may also be used as a bridle decoration, is likewise traceable to an Old World origin; on the other hand, the same form was known to the ancient Pueblos, for ornaments of this shape are found in ruin sites.

Silver bow guards were formerly made for use by the Navaho, and they may still be worn as ornaments. The practical need for the *ketoh* was to protect the wrist when using the bow and arrow. They may well serve in that capacity today, with the archery enthusiast, or as an unusual wrist ornament for dress occasions – particularly with evening wear – or with sport attire. As to the conchas (*concha* is the Spanish word for shell), the silver discs secured on leather belts, some authorities feel that it has been conclusively demonstrated that the Navaho derived them from the Plains Indians, their traditional enemies, such as the Ute,

ANTIQUES

WILSON
GALLERIES

direct importers

*Specializing in Pre-Columbian Art
of the West Coast Cultures*

400 CANYON ROAD, SANTA FE, NEW MEXICO

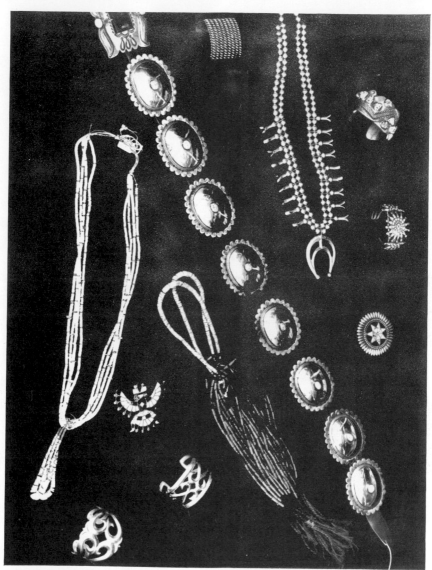

Choice examples of Indian jewelry: The hammered silver concha belt in the center is typically Navaho, as are the "squash blossom" necklace and large - set turquoise and silver bracelet to the right of it, and the two sandcast bracelets at the lower left. Coral necklaces, with or without turquoise pendants, are worn by Navaho and Pueblo alike. The shell and turquoise necklace is common to the Pueblo; the Navaho also adopted its use. The bracelets and pins with small turquoise sets, and the Knife Wing God of channel work, are representative of Zuñi styles.

Kiowa, and Comanche. On the contrary, since conchas identical with those found on old Navaho belts are made as bridle ornaments throughout Mexico, and by the Arabs on the southern edge of the Sahara desert, others think that their Old World derivation is certain.

Until about 1880, no settings of any kind were made. Then bits of glass, beads, buttons, and native garnets and jet began to be used. Turquoise was not set in quantity much before 1900. No symbols are represented by the designs stamped and engraved on Navaho jewelry; most of them are the same as those used for centuries by the Spanish and Mexican leather workers. Of course, innovations occur.

The French *Palmes Academiques* was awarded to Ambrose Roanhorse, in 1954, for outstanding production of Navaho silver work.

The Pueblo Indians, as well as the Navaho, are masters in jewelry making. They have known the art of carving turquoise, shell, and other substances, for centuries. Of the Pueblos, the people of Zuñi rank foremost in the production of jewelry. Their work in metals also started with the use of iron. About 1830 – 1840, they began to fashion jewelry from brass and copper. Old pots and pans, melted and hammered into shape, became buttons, rings, bracelets, and bow guard mountings. Later, copper and brass wire were used. Around 1870, the Zuñi learned from the Navaho how to work silver and make dies. When silver was introduced, working in brass and copper gradually died out for the most part.

During the 1870's and 1880's, Zuñi silver was simple and massive, like that of the Navaho. After the Zuñi learned to set turquoise, about 1890, their craft became increasingly complex in design. Until about 1920, the silver output of the Zuñi smiths was sold or traded entirely to Indians of that or other pueblos or to the Navaho. Then the traders began buying their jewelry for the tourist trade. At that time there were not over eight silversmiths at Zuni. Today there are hundreds; practically every man, woman, and child learned the art during the days of World War II, and the amount of production was astounding. Popular modern designs found in Zuñi jewelry include Knife Wing and Dragon Fly figures; men and women dressed in Zuñi attire; deer, butterflies, and other realistic figures in flat relief work. There is some carving in the round, as of fetishes.

Speaking generally, it is easy to distinguish Zuñi from Navaho silver – though it may be impossible to correctly identify individual pieces. With Zuñi jewelry, emphasis is on the *turquoise*; almost every piece shows many small, individually set stones, or channel work in larger stones. Zuñi silver pieces are of lighter weight than those of the Navaho. With the Navaho, it is the *silver* that counts most, and the turquoise settings are secondary. Almost every piece of Navaho workmanship shows stamped designs, but the Zuñi smith uses dies most sparingly, if at all. There are other minor differences which may aid one in telling Zuñi jewelry from the Navaho. Now, many Navaho wear jewelry made by the Zuñi Indians.

Some Hopi silverwork has been done since the latter part of the 19th century, having received its inspiration from Zuñi and Navaho smiths. In 1938 the Museum of Northern Arizona made silver manufacture among the Hopi one of its major projects. Hopi designs were utilized and distinctive pieces produced. Today, Hopi silverwork stands on its own merits.

Several of the other pueblos have a history of silver working which dates back roughly to 1890. Acoma and Isleta had a few silversmiths in the early days. Now, some of the younger people have learned this craft in school or in shops in the cities. The Laguna Indians have known silversmithing since 1870 or earlier. Among the Rio Grande villages, the Santo Domingo people make more jewelry than the other Indians. The silver craft has been known there since 1893. Santo Domingo silver jewelry is essentially an imitation of the Navaho. But the traditional jewelry of this pueblo consists of necklaces made of small disc beads of shell or turquoise; of shell beads and chunk turquoise; of jet – plain or inlaid with turquoise – and turquoise; and jet, shell, and turquoise mosaic. These necklaces often have a crescent pendant of jet or shell inlaid with turquoise. In recent years, though the necklace form has changed little, jet has given way to the similar appearing materials afforded by old phonograph records or battery cases; shell has largely been superseded by cylindrical beads made of gypsum; and shell and turquoise mosaic work has frequently been replaced by red-dyed gypsum and teeth from colored plastic combs.

Such necklaces, together with rings, bracelets, and various types of Indian jewelry, may often be purchased from itinerant Pueblo traders on the streets of Santa Fe and Albuquerque. The Indians, primarily Santo Domingo men, carry two or three blankets over the left shoulder, and hold their wares, invitingly, in either hand. Dressed more or less in Pueblo attire, with a colorful kerchief about the head or the hair done up in traditional *chongo* (French, *chignon*), these traders add a colorful note to the cities' throng.

Santa Ana and Jemez took up silversmithing about 1890, when they learned the craft from the Navaho. Santa Clara had taken up this style of jewelry making a few years earlier. There are several Cochiti silversmiths, most of whom work in Santa Fe. There are probably a few silversmiths in each of the pueblos.

THE GENUINE VS. THE IMITATION*

The buyer of all Indian arts and crafts items needs to exercise caution, and particularly with regard to jewelry. Unfortunately, things are not always what they seem. For this reason, the Southwestern Association on Indian Affairs carefully selects the advertising presented in this book, and recommends the dealers represented.

Most dealers are honest and conscientious, but a large quantity of so-called Indian arts and crafts is commercially manufactured and sold as of genuine Indian make, in many parts of the country, and particularly in the Southwest.

If you want a truly *handmade* Indian article, be sure to inquire about its authenticity. Some Indians are employed by commercial establishments in the manufacture of jewelry, and some do make such items in part, but when the Association uses the term *genuine Indian handmade* it means jewelry that an Indian silversmith fashions with his own hands with tools of his own, and using real silver – not stainless steel or nickel-plated copper.

In order to distinguish the genuine from the imitation, it is suggested that you take these three simple precautionary measures: find out about the reliability of the firm or the individual with whom you are dealing; in buying a piece of jewelry, be especially wary of perfection! In a handmade piece, neither the silver work nor the setting is perfect. Examine the materials carefully; even an untrained eye can usually tell the difference between a semi-precious turquoise and a reconstucted or imitation stone.

To be classified as authentic, an article must have a high sterling silver content, (today, nearly all handmade silver pieces are sterling), and the stone, if turquoise, must be genuine and unaltered. In most imitation pieces, the mounting is copper-plated with nickel, and the stone is plastic or altered turquoise.

In a genuine Zuñi channel inlay piece, the materials (turquoise, shell, coral, jet, etc.) are cut and laid into silver partitions, leaving a slight metal break between the setting and the partition. In imitation articles, materials resembling settings are poured in, leaving no break. And in the imitation pieces, the blue is too blue for turquoise, the red is too red for coral or shell, and the white is too white.

The sawtooth bezel (housing for a setting) on an imitation piece does not really grasp the setting, as it does in a Zuñi piece of cluster work. The spurious article is cast in a mold, after which the setting or stone is glued in.

A Navaho imitation setting has a vinyl tile effect, and the metal in a fake Navaho bracelet has no ring to it when struck with a hard object. Morever, the design around the stone is obviously pressed out, rather than soldered to horizontal bands as it would be on a genuine Indian-made bracelet. A machine-made bracelet never has the design stamped as deeply as a handmade article.

A sure test for determining the validity of the silver in a piece of jewelry is with nitric acid. Sterling silver turns white when the acid is applied; coin silver will be a little darker than sterling; Mexican silver may vary from a high silver content to very low, and the coloring from the acid reaction will vary from white for high silver content to dark for lower content. Nickel-plated copper in imitation jewelry will turn green.

There are laws in New Mexico and Colorado that require imitation Indian jewelry to be so labeled, but there are no means for enforcing them. Thus, one has to rely on reputable traderr and merchants or his own good judgement.

An Indian craftsman turns out a piece of authentic jewelry slowly and laboriously. Assembly-line jewelry can be manufactured and turned out by the hundreds in the time it takes an Indian craftsman to make one piece. The Indians cannot begin to compete with the manufacturer of Indian jewelry, but the uninformed buyer often pays almost as much, or as much, for the imitation as for the genuine. Silversmithing and other Indian crafts provide a livelihood for many Indians; they are important sources of income for the Indians.

The Association urges you to know what you are buying, and to buy the genuine. It is essential to the preservation of the traditional in Indian arts and crafts. You are justified in feeling proud of genuine Indian jewelry. It is truly beautiful, and many honest Indians, through many years, have been proud to make it so you might wear it.

A Navaho silversmith demonstrating the simple equipment with which he works: elementary forge (in basin at left) and bellows, anvil mounted in a wooden box, and a few tools and dies at his side. With these, he can produce a variety of beautiful jewelry. Behind the smith is a good example of a Two Grey Hills rug.

RESERVATION CRAFTS

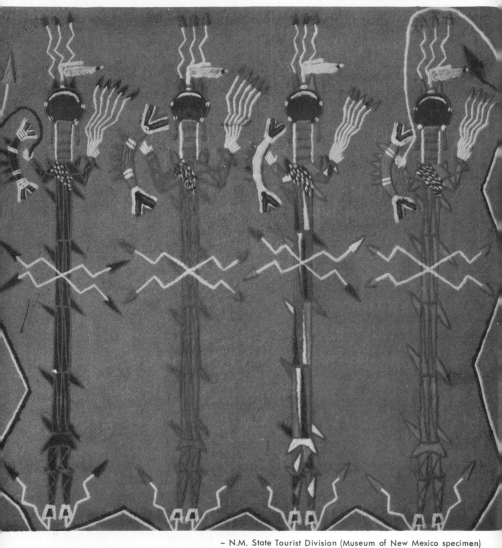

– N.M. State Tourist Division (Museum of New Mexico specimen)

One of four symbolic sandpaintings of the Female Shooting Chant of the Navaho. The colors derive from pulverized rocks native to the reservation; these are placed on a background of natural sand. Four Yei are represented.

PAINTINGS

Countless artistic records of the Indians of the Southwest are pecked, incised, or painted on the rocks – petroglyphs and pictographs. Pottery, from prehistoric times to the present, shows an extensive array of art forms. Occasionally, kiva paintings from ruin sites are uncovered. Fine examples of these wall paintings were found at Kuaua, an ancient pueblo near Bernalillo, New Mexico, now the Coronado State Monument. The kiva walls were found to have been covered with at least eighty-five layers of thin plaster, seventeen of which were decorated in true fresco painting. The kiva was restored, and the walls painted with replicas of the original frescoes. Other examples of these ancient works of art are shown in the Kuaua museum.

Archaeologists of the University of New Mexico have recently unearthed beautiful kiva paintings at Pottery Mound, a prehistoric pueblo on the Rio Puerco, southwest of Los Lunas. Some of these are similar to the Kuaua murals, others are very much like those excavated by Peabody Museum of Harvard University at Awatovi, in northeastern Arizona.

When the Indians decorate their pottery or weave rugs of intricate patterns, they do not first draw the design and measure the space as would a white artist, yet the pattern of a good artist never fails to come out even and well balanced. Another example of sure eye and steady hand is illustrated by the Navaho sandpaintings. The "painters" often start at opposite sides of the large picture and without any previous marking of spaces come together in the completed design. According to most authorities, the Navaho learned the art of sandpainting from the Pueblos, who still make drypaintings during some of their ceremonies. The Jicarilla Apache and Pima use drypaintings in some of their rituals.

In Santa Fe, the Museum of Navaho Ceremonial Art makes a special exhibition of Navaho sandpaintings. It has a collection of about eight hundred copies in color of sandpainting designs. As mentioned above, visitors do not often have an opportunity to witness the making of sandpaintings inside a ceremonial hogan, but this art may be observed at the Inter-tribal Ceremonial at Gallup in mid-August of each year, and at the Museum of Northern Arizona, Flagstaff, during certain special exhibitions.

Early in this century, a few of the Indian School teachers and other individuals began to take an interest in the drawings that certain young Indians produced when given colored crayons or water colors and paper. Miss Elizabeth J. Richards did much to encourage pupils in the San Ildefonso day school to draw the dance figures and to make cut-out patterns in colored papers, using Indian designs. Among these young artists showing promise were *Wen' Tsireh* and *Awa Tsireh* (Alfredo Montoya and Alfonso Roybal respectively). In 1910, the late Dr. E. L. Hewett noticed that one of the boys helping with the excavations at El Rito de los Frijoles was "dabbling with water color paints." It proved to be Alfredo. He was further encouraged and provided with suitable materials. Soon he was painting pictures which his white friends were glad to purchase. Unfortunately the young artist died in 1913. But he had influenced others at San

Ildefonso.

A cousin of Alfredo's, Cresencio Martinez, according to the custom of that pueblo, was painting designs on the pottery made by the womenfolk of his family. Then he began making water color paintings. In 1917, he announced to Dr. Hewett that he could paint all of the costumed figures in their ceremonial dances. He was given supplies, and promptly made good his claim. His work attracted the favorable attention of eminent artists. But he, too, was destined for an early death, in 1918.

Within a short time after Cresencio began painting ceremonial figures, other Indian boys made it known that they also could paint pictures. One of these was Awa Tsireh. Another was a Hopi boy, Fred Kabotie. There was Otis Polelonema, also a Hopi; and *Ma-pe-wi,* or Velino Shije Herrera, of Zia. These young men, inspired by Cresencio's example and by the appreciation accorded his work, showed the same singular talent which he possessed. There was never any experimentation with their colors or patterns. Each picture was mentally completed, then with elaborate precision in drawing and color it was skillfully executed.

In 1919, there was an exhibit of Indian water colors in the Arts Club of Chicago. Three years later, the School of American Research in Santa Fe employed Awa Tsireh, Velino, and Kabotie to paint a few hours each day; no one instructed or influenced them, but their work during the period has never been excelled for color and composition. Velino appears to have been the first to introduce the element of pure design into Pueblo water color painting. At the same time, he was painting beautiful, action-filled horses in a masterly way. He continued to produce excellent works thoughout the years, until an auto wreck on Christmas eve, 1956, incapacitated him extensively. Kabotie has painted less, but has taught arts and crafts among his people to this day. Polelonema was inactive for many years, while raising and educating a family, but now has resumed his art. Awa Tsireh painted hundreds of pictures until his death, in March, 1955. The day before he died, he was in Santa Fe to get paper for more paintings. One of the first young women to attract attention by her artistic production was the late Tonita Peña, a San Ildefonso girl married to a Cochiti man. Many dealers have the works of these artists for sale, and museums all over the country exhibit their pictures.

Indian art is as distinct from European or American art as is Chinese or Japanese, to which Indian art is more nearly related. It is decorative and imaginative, usually two-dimensional, although the Hopi and other individuals have painted in the round. There is seldom a background, but a few recent painters have indicated backgrounds in a simple, thoroughly original, but satisfying manner. Sacred subjects such as rain, the rainbow, and clouds are represented symbolically. Indians do not paint from models; because of their powers of observation and memory they have no need for them. Traditionally, more important objects may be made larger or more prominent. In some ways, it may be said that Indian art is four-dimensional; they actually paint the rhythm and steps of the dance, the action of the horse, the speed of the antelope, the heat of the desert.

As late as 1928, it was the general practice to forbid the painting of Indian subjects in the government Indian schools. But, in 1932, the Bureau of Indian Affairs established a painting department in the Santa Fe Indian School, and placed it under the inspired direction of Miss Dorothy Dunn (now Mrs. Max Kramer) — inspired, because instead of teaching in the conventional manner, she taught the Indians about the great arts of the world, and showed that the art of every nation had declined as it imitated the art of other nations. She gave her students pride and confidence in their own traditions, and instruction only in the use of white men's tools. She left her students free to develop their imaginations and techniques as racial instinct led them. Five years later, Mrs. Kramer was succeeded at the School by one of her own talented pupils, Geronima Cruz (Mrs. Juan Montoya) of the pueblo of San Juan. Some good paintings were also produced in the Albuquerque Indian School at that time. One of the outstanding artists to come from that institution was José Rey Toledo of Jemez, but he no longer paints.

Each year, exhibitions of Indian paintings from the Santa Fe Indian School were held in museums all over the United States and in many foreign countries, including galleries in London and Paris. The department was not only self-supporting through the sales of student work (paying 50 per cent to the artists), but it also contributed to other school activities. In 1940, one of the students, Ben Quintana of Cochiti pueblo, won the Youth Administration prize of $1,000, over more than fifty thousand contestants from all parts of the United States. In 1951, Vidal Casiquito, Jr., Jemez, was one of twelve winners in a poster contest sponsored by the National Cartoonist Society and the U. S. Treasury. Indian artists have won many honors and awards.

After about a decade of outstanding artistic productions by students in the art department, the war's demands on the young people, changes in policy at the Santa Fe School, and a variety of factors – far beyond Mrs. Montoya's control – resulted in an apalling degeneracy of Indian art. There are, fortunately, a few of the prewar artists who still produce fine works, such as Gilbert Atencio of San Ildefonso; Theodore Suina and Joe H. Herrera of Cochiti; Pablita Velarde Hardin, Santa Clara; and Harrison Begay, Narciso Abeyta (Ha-So-De), and Jimmie Toddy (Beatien Yazz), Navaho. Among the Apache artists are Allan Houser, Rudolph Treas, Emmet Botella, and Frank Vigil now living at Jemez. Houser's sculpturing also commands considerable attention. He and Fred Kabotie have both been honored by the Guggenheim Foundation, each receiving fellowships to continue their art work. When the *Palmes Academiques* were presented to Indian artists, in 1954, those recognized for their paintings were: Fred Kabotie, Joe H. Herrera, Pablita Velarde, Harrison Begay, Allan Houser, Awa Tsireh, Velino Herrera, and Andrew Tsihnahjinnie, a Navaho painter from Arizona. Although too busy with teaching most of the time to produce much of her own work, Mrs. Montoya is an accomplished artist who has had noteworthy exhibitions.

Of those who took up painting af-

Water color painting by Ma-pe-wi (Velino Herrera) of Buffalo dancers

– photo by Ernest Knee

ter war service, Joe V. Aguilar, San Ildefonso, continues his art work. It is regrettable that there are so few on-coming artists at the present time, and that many talented ones are too occupied with other modes of livelihood to produce any paintings. Among the younger artists of promise are: Sylvia Vicenti, Jicarilla Apache; Pete Gaspar, Roger Tsabetsaye, and Dixon Shebala, Zuñi; Thomas Montoya, San Juan; Christino Peña, San Ildefonso; and Gibson Talahytewa and Roderick Holmes, Hopi. Other Hopi artists now painting, include Poliyesva, Bruce Timeche, and Robert Preston.

Here, it should be noted that another era at the United States Indian School in Santa Fe has come to a close. The school, as such, has ceased to educate Indian students through high school grades and, thus, to follow the former program of instruction in aboriginal arts. This change was followed by establishment of the Institute of American Indian Art, which opened in October, 1962, in remodeled quarters of the Santa Fe school, and has since built new structures.

A stated purpose of the Institute is to "open new doors of opportunity for self-expression (of young Indians from Federally recognized groups, with at least one-quarter Indian blood) in the whole rainbow of the arts." A comprehensive academic program of studies for selected art-interested students is offered in grades 10 through 12. That is, the high school program is intended to "meet the needs of art students preparing for fine arts work in college, art students preparing for technical schools, art students completing their formal education upon graduation from high school."

For students desiring work in advance of the 12th grade, a two-year program of specialized studies is offered. The arts courses encompass fine arts and crafts (painting, sculpturing, ceramics, textile arts), and dramatic arts (including creative writing, dramatics, dancing, and music). Related courses include business training and mathematics, English, history, applied science, typing, etc.

The Institute started with a small student body. The second year saw enrollment increased to 140. Familiar names appear on the faculty roster, such as Lloyd New (Kiva), Allan Houser, and Charles and Otellie Loloma from Hopiland.

At the recent Scottsdale (Arizona) National Indian Arts Exhibition, Mrs. Loloma (Otellie) won the Charles de Y. Elkus Memorial award for a bronze of a Hopi child, and a first prize of $100 in the sculpture and woodcarving classification. Narcisco Abeyta, Navaho artist, won a special award of $125 in the water-based painting category; the $75 first prize was awarded Gilbert Atencio, San Ildefonso. Two other Navaho gained awards: Carl Gorman won the $75 first place in paintings with new vistas; Harry Walters won the Governor's Trophy and $50 in special competition. An honor mention, the only award presented in the experimental classification, went to Pablita Velarde, Santa Clara artist.

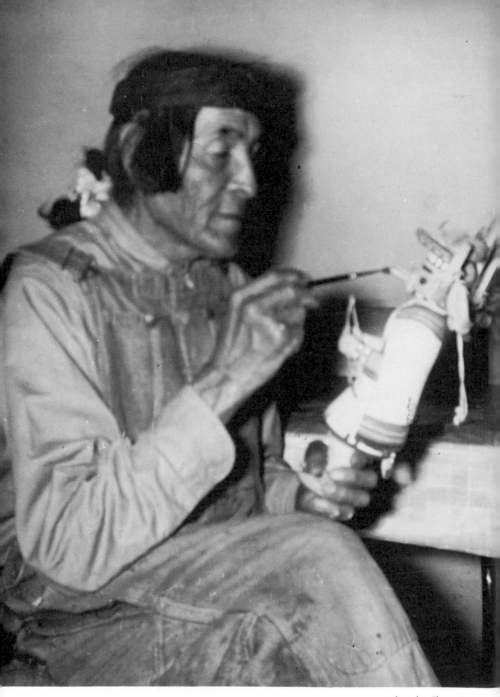

Peter Nuvamsa, Sr., Second Mesa Hopi, painting a katsina which he has carved

Mention has been made of the importance of the katsina cult in Pueblo social organization (*see* p. 17). Not only may *katsina* refer to supernatural beings and to their human personators, but to wooden figurines as well. The term is in general use among the Pueblo peoples, though the connotation may vary, and each language accounts for diverse pronunciations and numerous spellings. It is to be remembered that none of the Indians had a written language, prior to the coming of the Europeans; consequently, the recordings of Indian words have followed systems devised outside of the aboriginal groups.

The word, katsina (ka - AH - tsin-ah), is believed to be of Keresan origin; the Hopi pronunciation differs a little (cot - SEE - nah).

The small wooden representations of katsinas are commonly called "dolls." They are not dolls as non-Indians think of them, as toys. They are likenesses of a whole array of supernaturals who, through various manifestations, interact between man and his deity; thus they are messengers. As such, they may appear in numerous forms, with specific identifying characteristics. This class of katsina representations has a separate designation within the Indian groups. For instance, the Hopi call them *tihü* or *katsıntihü*. While they are not playthings, it is not considered wrong if an Indian child carries one of them about, as a non-Indian youngster might carry a doll.

Primarily, the katsinas are benevolent beings who reside in the mountains, clouds, springs and lakes, and who are purveyors of many blessings, especially rain, good crops, and general well being. However, as all good has its contrary agency, some katsinas are ogres or demons with disciplinary functions. Ogres have a reputation for eating children if they are not good, and if the katsinas are not obeyed. Indian lore and social mores are transmitted from generation to generation by means of the katsinas. In many ways, the supernatural ones and the katsina organizations reflect the ordinary life of the Pueblo peoples; the family relationship is the same: father, mother, children, grandparents, uncles, and so on.

In further explanation of the little wooden figures, faithfully portrayed, it has been noted that they provide a means of education; they also serve as gifts at ceremonials, and as decorative articles in the home; but, transcendently, they act as a constant reminder to the Indians of the "real" katsinas.

Not all of the figurines represent katsinas. How, then, does one distinguish them? Although it is sometimes difficult to determine, the essential feature is the mask. Unmasked figures are *not* katsinas. Examples of these are Buffalo, Deer, Eagle, and Snake dancers, etc.

Another expression of Indian art, consequently, is to be seen in the carved wooden figures of katsinas or ceremonial personages. Here, the Hopi Indians take lead, for religious restrictions in the Rio Grande valley do not allow profane production of ceremonial figures. James Kewanwytewa, a Hopi Indian well known at the Museum of Northern Arizona, in Flagstaff, won the *Palmes Academiques* for his katsina productions, in 1954. Although many katsinas, or dolls, are offered for sale, one has to be careful that he is securing authentic specimens, for non-Indians are making many imitations.

If made in traditional Hopi manner, katsina figures are carved from a solid piece of root wood from a dead cottonwood tree; for this reason, they are of a very light weight. They should be so well balanced as to stand alone. Protruding eyes, ears, and nose, horns, and headdress ornaments may be attached with tiny pegs. Clothing and costume articles are indicated by painting. First, a coat of very fine white clay, called kaolin, is applied over all of the figure. Then colored pigments are laid on. Formerly these were native earth or mineral colors. Today, water color or paints are commonly used.

The Zuñi style, and that of some of the Rio Grande Pueblos, calls for the use of pine wood for katsina figures. These are then painted, and are dressed in costumes of deerskin, fur, feathers, and cloth – minature replicas of the human size beings. Zuñi "dolls" are generally taller, more slender, and heavier in weight than the Hopi figures, and they usually have movable arms. They do not stand without support, as a rule.

A Hopi carving of the Hémis *katsina, a very popular and highly symbolic figure. The supernatural represented appears in the Regular Katsina Dances, which may be part of one-day or nineday ceremonies; these impersonators are frequently seen in the* Nimán *or Home Dance which the Hopi give in July, when the katsinas "go home" to the San Francisco peaks north of Flagstaff, Arizona.*

– photo by Laura Gilpin
(Museum of New Mexico specimen)

Visitors who are fortunate enough to be in Santa Fe during the summer months and over Labor Day, will find that the Indians and their products under the portal of the Palace of the Governors make a picturesque spectacle. There purchases may be made directly from the Indians.

Early in the morning on market days, the Indians, carrying their wares wrapped in pieces of calico or packed into paper cartons, come into town and arrange themselves for the day. Their backs to the wall, they sit either on the sidewalk or on low stools. When the back row is filled the full length of the block, a second row forms along the curb. In front of them, the Indians spread their pottery, drums – both full-size and toy – dressed dolls, jewelry, baskets, moccasins, tanned goat skins, paintings, beaded trinkets, textiles, and unpredictable articles. Indians are imaginative and inventive, and each year they come forth with new examples of their productive minds.

Usually the price is fixed for items sold in the Indian markets, though sometimes the Indians enjoy a little bargaining. But be perfectly sure that the Indians are quite as shrewd as you are. They will not sell for less than an article is worth.

At the annual Inter-tribal Indian Ceremonial in Gallup, fine weaving, jewelry, pottery, paintings, basketry, moccasins and other leather goods, and miscellaneous Indian products, are assembled from many of the Indian groups and are judged for merit by experts. Most of the articles exhibited are for sale.

Colorful fairs are held in the Navaho country during the autumn season, usually at Shiprock, New Mexico, and Window Rock, Arizona. Visitors will do well to attend either or both of these events. The New Mexico State Fair at Albuquerque in late September, and the Arizona State Fair in Phoenix in early November, have exhibits of Indian arts and crafts which are for sale. Annually, the Museum of Northern Arizona centers a Hopi Arts and Crafts show around July 4, when thousands of the Hopi and Western Navaho, as well as their New Mexico neighbors, gather at Flagstaff.

Off of the highways are trading posts which handle Indian products. Throughout the Navaho country, certain trading posts, or booths, exhibit Navaho rugs and other items to attract the traveler. With the Navaho goods one may also find Chimayó textiles for sale. These are fine in their own way, but they definitely are *not* Indian. They are made by the Spanish - American weavers in their small villages in the upper Rio Grande drainage. Trading posts in Arizona and Colorado handle more Hopi and Papago items, and wares of other groups.

For the traveler who has limited knowledge of Indian arts and crafts, it is recommended that he do his buying from established dealers throughout the four - state region. Their trained buyers make frequent trips to the reservations or pueblos and select the best. They often have arrangements with craftsmen of particular skill to take their entire output, or they have expert Indian workmen in their own shops.

Colorful display of handicraft at the Santa Fe Indian market in front of the Palace of the Governors — photo by Laura Gilpin

The Changing Indian*

Visitors to New Mexico, after an absence of some years, find the Indian pueblos little changed externally, but are surprised by the altered appearance of many of the people, particularly those whom they meet on the streets of towns surrounding the pueblos. Gone are the colorful blankets formerly worn by the men, replaced now by leather coats; only a few bright headbands are seen. The young men no longer need the headbands for they have not let their hair grow since the wartime services. Switches of long black hair to be worn in the dances may be found in the Indian trading posts.

Even the more conservative women, except the very old, have given up the wearing of shawls, and no young girl would think of appearing except in the standardized dress and hair-do of non-Indian girls her age. A few of the most conservative Pueb-

* This section was originally prepared by the late Margretta S. Dietrich, who long served this Association on Indian Affairs as its president, and who was ever a friend to the Indians.

-- photo by James Bosch

A Navaho "long hair" placing his vote in a ballot box (note the skill-fully arranged chongo *below his hat brim)*

lo Councils still insist on the wearing of typical Indian costumes at home. A recent governor of Taos, who himself still adheres to the blanket and moccasins, recently said regretfully, "Pretty soon you won't be able to tell an Indian from anyone else without a blood test." He was not aware that there is no difference between Indian and non-Indian blood – except as individual blood types may differ.

Many Indian brides now wear white satin and veils for their weddings, but they are still blessed by the old ladies of the family with a touch on the shoulder and a scattering of sacred corn meal.

Within the houses of the Pueblo Indians, the changes are startling. Most of the pueblos now have electricity under the Rural Electrification Administration and the Indians have been quick to install not only lights but refrigerators, radios, deep freezes, washing machines and television sets. Installment buying has also been accepted, and small loan concerns enjoy an extensive business with the Indian people.

Several pueblos now have sewer systems, and have water in every house. Modern construction blocks frequently take the place of adobe bricks or native rock in new dwellings. The Navaho are considering tapping the gas lines which cross their reservation for cooking and heating in the hogans. More stone hogans and more windows and real doors have made their appearance on the reservation in the last few years. Some hogans have venetian blinds, and many have overstuffed furniture and sewing machines. Ornamental screen doors are especially favored by the Pueblos, and steel window frames are winning favor.

Twenty-five years ago few Indians owned or drove cars. Now it is a common sight to see Indian women driving, and many drive heavy trucks with the same ease as their men.

Although there have been changes throughout the years, and "integration" with non-Indian society is on the way, Indians still retain the essence of their culture, which we hope will continue indefinitely. As a minority group, they need the protection of non-Indian citizens of good will against the greed of those non-Indians who rationalize that Indians living in our society should have no special federal protections since they are now full-fledged voting citizens. These protections were promised the Indians in consideration for the lands taken from them.

Since 1948, when the Indians of New Mexico and Arizona were enfranchised, some of the Pueblo councils have ordered their people not to register for voting because they fear they will next have to pay property taxes; but each election sees more attention given to the matter of voting. The Navaho have registered in great numbers and well realize their political force as citizens.

The Navaho have a democratically elected Tribal Council, with elections being held every four years. The last one was held in March, 1963, when Raymond Nakai was elected chairman. Nakai seeks to establish on the reservation vocational schools and livestock associations to protect the sheep growers; he wants the setting up of small businesses to hire Navaho employees. Campaigning before elections is active. Voters, both men and women over twenty-one, must register; voting is done by ballot on which the candidates' pho-

tographs as well as names are printed for the benefit of the illiterate. Women can and do serve on the Council.

All officers are sworn in by a District Judge from Arizona or New Mexico. Uniformed and trained Navaho police are selected by the Advisory Committee, which is comparable to the Cabinet of the United States.

Window Rock, Arizona, close to the New Mexico border, is the Navaho "capital." The Council House

A Navaho Tribal Council inauguration at Window Rock, Arizona

is octagonal, like a huge hogan. Each member of the Council has a desk with his name on it. Meetings are now conducted entirely by the Navaho; Indian Service personnel are available for consultation but do not participate unless requested. The offices and sandstone residences, originally built for Indian Service personnel, have been taken over almost entirely by the Navaho, and many modern dwellings have been built. The Navaho-Zuñi area office has been moved to Gallup where a $200,000 building has been erected and leased for its headquarters.

Pueblo Councils retain more of their old characteristics – great decorum is maintained, and visitors may attend only on special invitation. The Council is also Court in many pueblos.

The All Pueblo Council, where common problems are discussed, is composed of representatives from each pueblo. One change is noted – no longer are interpreters used; English is the language. If a delegation needs an interpreter it must bring its own.

Legislation

An Act was passed by the 83rd Congress, now known as Public Law 280, which allows states which accept its provisions to assume criminal and civil jurisdiction over Indian tribes. New Mexico and Arizona have taken no action as yet on the subject. Indians opposed this law because if state laws applied on their reservations, it would take judicial authority from their tribal governments – authority which they have exercised since time immemorial, a right which was confirmed rather than granted under the Reorganization Act of 1934. Their tribal courts, differing somewhat in each tribe or pueblo, all have jurisdiction over minor offenses. The federal government has jurisdiction over ten major crimes, such as murder, manslaughter, rape, arson, etc.

If the states assumed the power authorized in Public Law 280, Indian marriage, divorce, inheritance customs, among other things, would be changed and many minor cases such as irrigation disputes and ownership matters would be thrown into the already over-crowded state courts. It would bankrupt poor counties which already have insufficient personnel in the sheriffs' offices, or there would be no enforcement at all in Indian country.

State jurisdiction over law and order will come gradually, without doubt, but it should not be forced on Indians against their will. Indians have accepted voluntarily many of our customs without compulsion and without being hurried. If we believe in self-determination for other peoples, we should also believe in it for Indians.

Many other bills have been introduced in recent sessions of Congress which would abolish the Indian Bureau and make the states responsible for administering Indian affairs. New Mexico and Arizona are too poor to assume the cost of Indian administration; without federal assistance, Indians would become a heavy welfare problem in these states.

Indians are facing the grave problem of settling the heirship of divided allotted land. The original allotments of 160 acres each have since been cut up to such an extent through inheritance that the fractions are of no practical value to the heirs or anyone else. Safeguards should be set up whereby co-owners or the tribe will have the first option to buy these pieces of land which are now being bought up by non-Indians with ready cash. Arrangements should also be made to lend money to the co-owners or tribe to purchase this land at a reasonable figure if they do not have funds available for this purpose.

The discovery of oil and rich minerals on Indian land has made it valuable to the Indian owner and to the non-Indian who covets it. It is important that the Indian be protected and that he receive guidance in granting leases and in the use of revenue, for which he has received no preparation in former years.

Health

Public Law 568, which was passed in the first session of the 83rd Congress, transferred health services for Indians to the U. S. Public Health Service, taking it from the Bureau of Indian Affairs and putting it in the U. S. Department of Health, Education and Welfare. The Act, at that time, was opposed by New Mexico Pueblo Indians because they feared that the new department would not understand their needs and problems, but with the statement of plans by the Public Health Service for more hospitals and clinics and more nurses, they became hopeful. The announcement that Indian hospitals would not be closed, and that there might be ambulance service, tended to reassure them.

Already there has been great improvement in health facilities to the Indians, but in spite of this Indian health conditions contrast sharply with those of the general population. The average age at death among the Pueblos is 42.5 years, and with the Navaho, 27.7 years, compared to 48.7 years among the population of New Mexico as a whole. In this state, 26 per cent of Pueblo Indian deaths, and 36 per cent of those of the Navaho, occur before the fifth year; and there is five times as much tuberculosis and ten times as much enteric disease among Indians as non-Indians. Trachoma increased at a startling rate in recent years, after having been practically wiped out by the sulfa drugs.

The U. S. Public Health Service has a contract with the University of Pennsylvania Medical School to conduct research among Indian pueblos in preventive diseases for children, and has contracts in effect with state agencies for the care of tubercular patients. It estimates that one-half of the deaths among Indians are from diseases that can be prevented or controlled, and it is working with Indians in their communities on this problem. The professional staff members carry on educational work with the families of the patient as well as with school children and community leaders. Field nurses now give their attention to whole families when they make home visits. There is preventive dental care for school children in many localities, and medical social work has increased greatly in recent years. Tuba City has a 75 bed hospital, as does Shiprock; Crownpoint has 56 beds, and the new hospital at Gallup, 200; Zuñi has a 39 bed hospital, the Mescalero, 25; and the Indian hospital in Santa Fe, 38.

Water

It is interesting to see the change of attitude of Indians toward water;

Traditionally, illness among the Indians was treated by their medicine men and medicine women. Curing ceremonies often extended over several days and nights. Accompanying the curative rites were chants and dancing; the "sings" attracted visitors from far and near. Shown here are dancers and chanters of the Mountain Top Way of the Navaho (see page 49), appearing at the Inter-tribal Indian Ceremonial at Gallup, New Mexico.

when wells were first drilled in some of the pueblos, they were promptly filled in. Water is a sacred element and should not be brought through pipes. In Taos when the young men came back from war service, they wished to pipe water into their new homes built at a distance from the old pueblo. Their requests were denied by the Taos Council, and those who put water into their houses without permission were severely penalized. However, one of the first demands of many of the pueblos at the present time is for a greater supply of water for domestic use, which means the drilling of more wells and repairs to old windmills.

At Zuñi Pueblo a 1,700-foot well was drilled for irrigation purposes, and at the Zuñi village of Pescado four springs have been enlarged and cleaned to supply both domestic and irrigation water. One of the springs has been walled and covered, with a pump installed for domestic water. In the past the people of the village drank from an open ditch or large pool. Zuñi officials borrowed $70,000 to install domestic water systems, which also included bringing water into all the homes at Zuñi proper. The loan was to cover only the cost of material, as labor would be provided by the Zuñi themselves. Each family was assessed five dollars to retire the loan, which is now entirely repaid.

At the Gallup Indian Community Center established in Gallup in 1954, there are dormitory facilities for transient Indians at $1.00 per night, which are very well patronized. But even more popular than beds or recreation facilities are the baths. A shower may be enjoyed for fifteen cents, which includes a towel and a cake of soap. More than 17,000

Continued on page 130

A Navaho medicine man and his friend, the modern doctor

-- photo by Gene Price

Copper Mine chapter house construction on Navaho reservation

Texas Zinc Mill, where Navaho workmen, Billy Yellow and Elwood Fore (on hammer), display their skills with modern industrial equipment

baths were indulged in by Indians within the first six months.

Industry and Employment

A few Pueblo Indians have gone into business for themselves in their villages, opening stores, garages, and silversmith shops. Many are working away from their villages in all the trades, in business concerns, and in offices. There are licensed Pueblo electricians and plumbers, excellent tailors, competent secretaries, trained nurses, teachers, artists, etc. Navaho have gone into business in a big way. The tribe took over its sawmill, which was losing money under non-Indian management, but under their own management they are making money. They have constructed a large, very modern sawmill near Fort Defiance, which was planned to absorb the functions of the original mill. They have built motels which they operate on the reservation, and have plans for other enterprises. They own several trading posts, and manage the Navaho Arts and Crafts Guild.

Under the ten-year Long Range Program of 1950, Navaho were to be given all possible employment in all building operations or road construction on the reservation, but under an economy move of the Department of the Interior, all work is being let to the lowest bidder, who is a contractor with his own crew of workmen; Navaho are no longer given preference. Their employment was to have been part of an on-the-job training program, and it is understood that they were making excellent operators of heavy equipment, as well as competent craftsmen in all the building trades. It is unfortunate that the government is not living up

to its provisions in the Rehabilitation Act. However, private industry is utilizing many Navaho on mining projects, and other undertakings.

Also, the Tribal Council appropriated a substantial amount for industrial development on the reservation to provide employment for the Navaho; many are employed by the railroads and still more opportunities are opening up in the oil fields and uranium processing plants which are operating near Farmington and in the Four Corners Area. A ten-year lease was signed by the Navaho Tribe and the Utah Construction Company, on nearly 25,000 acres of Navaho land, for the construction of a huge multi-million dollar steam power generating plant on the banks of the San Juan river west of Farmington. This land, which is too barren for grazing, contains vast deposits of low quality coal which will be utilized to produce vital electric power for this entire area. The Utah Construction Company has agreed to furnish power at wholesale rates to the Navaho, who will be able to use it for industrial as well as domestic purposes, and will also benefit from the project in terms of employment in the construction and operation of the plant. The El Paso Natural Gas Company has leased nearly 100,000 acres in the Burnham area of the reservation, about 50 miles southwest of Farmington, New Mexico, for prospecting and possible development of a strip-mine operation. Explorations revealed some 519 million tons of strippable coal in the whole area. If El Paso's plan to convert the coal into motor fuel components and gaseous hydrocarbons proves feasible, up to 200 jobs will be provided, mainly for the Navaho.

The manual dexterity which most Indians possess, makes them skillful in modern industry as well as in their native arts and crafts. Navaho people are particularly adept at accepting new challenges. Here, two Navaho women, Curtie Dawes and Lucille Boone, demonstrate their expertness in an electronics factory which operated for a while near the Navaho reservation.

A western Navaho weaver seated before her loom in front of the family hogan, where she deftly manipulates the tools and yarns which enable her to produce a beautifully designed rug.

Job opportunities off the reservation have been facilitated by the Relocation Program of the Bureau of Indian Affairs which was set up in 1950 to assist Indians to find work elsewhere. Although far from perfect, this program has already helped thousands of Indian men, women, and children to make the adjustment from reservation or pueblo life to other localities.

During the spring of 1963, upward of $1 1/2 million were spent for improvements on fifteen New Mexico reservations, in accordance with the 1962 accelerated Public Works Act. The project areas covered were conservation, roads, and community buildings, which provided employment for approximately 645 Indians. Conservation, which included the clearing of range land of scrub brush, and building fences, was granted $622,400. Of this, the Acoma Indians were allotted $125,000; other Pueblo allotments were: Laguna $105,800, Jemez $36,300, Santo Domingo $55,300, San Ildefonso $25,000, Santa Clara $100,-000, San Juan $55,000, Taos $100,-000; to the Navaho, the Cañoncito and the Puertocito $10,000 each. Santa Clara was also granted $252,-000 for community water and sewer facilities; and Laguna $48,000.

Two groups received money for road improvements, Santa Clara $300,000 for seven miles of blacktop road, and Acoma $275,000 for construction of 12 miles of gravel-surface road.

New community buildings were budgeted for six pueblos. These were planned with a council meeting room, a detention room for men and women, an administration wing, an office for the pueblo governor, and toilet facilities. Location of these new structures and the cost thereof are: Isleta $68,000, Santo Domingo $47,000, Tesuque $25,000, Pojoaque $25,000, Nambé $30,000, and Picurís $30,000. Unaided, San Ildefonso built a community center and administration building.

In addition to the governmental projects, private industries are providing benefits for the Pueblo peoples. Laguna has secured an electronics plant which will employ 400 people, and eventually will have a payroll of $750,000. Sandía has leased land for the base of a proposed aerial tramway to Sandía Crest. This will yield $1,000 a year in rentals for the first three years and, thereafter, $7,500 per year plus a percentage of the gross income. Isleta is negotiating for a $300,000 canning factory, which would employ about fifteen people, and purchase farm products from the pueblo.

The Mescalero Apache have recently awarded a $66,791 contract for the improvement of the water and sewer system on their reservation. Plans are under way for construction of a fish hatchery on the reservation.

The Jicarilla Apache received a grant under the accelerated Public Works Act for $152,000 for improvement of their community water and sewer facilities.

The history of the federal government's treatment of Indians, on the whole, has not been one of which to be proud; excuses were found to justify any treatment. At one time it was thought that the Indians were a dying people, and would not need large reservations; it was argued that it would be better to sell much of their land and use the proceeds to "educate and civilize" such Indians as might survive.

Far from dying off, in the 1900 census, there were 39,624 Indians in Arizona and New Mexico. According to the 1950 census, 107,662 Indians lived in these two states. Today there are approximately 154,000. It is gratifying to see that the federal government is giving more heed to its obligations to the Indians; and it is encouraging and wholly satisfying to note how much the Indian peoples are doing for themselves, once they are given the assistance needed and educational privileges.

Education

Many changes are taking place in the attitudes of Indians. A few years ago all Southwestern Indian groups opposed the government's educational efforts. They did not want their children taken away to Indian boarding schools, but they opposed the building of Indian day schools to take care of the younger children in their home communities. Navaho opposed schools because they took the children away from herding sheep. Not many years ago, less than half the children of some of the larger pueblos were permitted by their parents to attend the day schools.

More Indian children are attending state schools each year, in spite of the fear on the part of some older members of the tribe that it will interfere with their religious training as Indians. Children are permitted to go home from the Pueblo Indian boarding schools to take part in religious dances and ceremonies, and a former principal of a day school, a man who was unusually understanding and sympathetic, each year asked the pueblo officials what boys they wanted to have kept out of school so that they might receive special religious instruction in their kivas. State attendance laws would not permit such practices. Unfortunately, the qualities we admire so greatly in Indians – their serenity and their fine spiritual balance – may be lost when Indian education has been placed under the states, but for economic reasons Indian parents feel forced to accept the risk. There is not enough land and not enough opportunity for all the people to make a living at home. The children must be prepared to compete in the outside world. At a conference on education held in Gallup, all the Indians agreed that "Indians need better education now; they are ready for it and cannot progress further without it." Unfortunately, the drop-out rate among the Indian children is 50 per cent higher than among non-Indians.

An illustration of the progress being made in education is seen at Zuñi where a sixteen-classroom Public High School was built in 1956, and negotiations were made to transfer to the Public School system all children in the elementary grades. This transfer became effective 1 September 1959, and the entire educational program at Zuñi is under the direct supervision of the McKinley county, New Mexico, Board of Education.

At present, over 80 percent of the Zuñi High School graduates avail themselves of opportunities in fields of higher education, which include vocations, commercial training, and college.

The Jicarilla Apache now have full grade and high school opportunities on the reservation and have set up a 20-year trust fund of $1,000,000, the income from which is to aid students in higher education either at the college level or for vocational

John E. Baker (seated) and David Box are among Southern Ute leaders. Baker was chairman of the planning committee which wrote the Southern Ute Rehabilitation Plan, has been a member of the Tribal Council since 1952 with the exception of one short period, and has been chairman of the Tribal Council since 1956 except for one year.

training.

A history-making event occurred recently at Dulce, when the Jicarilla Indians came to the aid of the white man. Until 1958, Jicarilla children were educated by the federal government on the reservation, or they attended small public schools in Dulce, Gobernador, and Lumberton. Then, an independent school district was organized. After nearly four years, the non-Indians of the district turned to the Indians for aid in building a much - needed school gymnasium. The Jicarilla erected a $200,000 structure, and the school district leased it for ten years, paying an annual rental of $25,000 plus 5.5 per cent interest. The all-steel gymnasium contains 20,000 feet of floor space and has a bleacher seating capacity of 1,400. The building was dedicated on 15 March 1963, with Indian and non-Indian dignitaries in attendance, including the Governor of New Mexico, who stated that this was, "the first occasion to my knowledge that an Indian tribe has used tribal funds to build and lease to a school district such an educational facility." More than 80 per cent of the school's 596 students enrolled in grades kindergarten through 12th are Indian; some 250 of these are housed in the Bureau of Indian Affairs boarding school dormitories adjacent to the classroom building.

When the Navaho-Hopi Rehabilitation Act was passed, it authorized $25,000,000 for schools and education facilities for Navaho children, out of a total authorization of $86,-000,000. At that time fewer than one hundred had ever attended a high school, and 80 per cent of the tribe was illiterate. Great progress has been made, particularly since 1954. Reservation day schools have been converted into boarding schools. New and enlarged dormitories have been built at old boarding schools, and several new school plants have been constructed. In addition, trailer schools have been placed at outlying locations on the reservation. Likewise, provisions have been made for boarding facilities in towns surrounding the reservation, to enable the children to attend public schools. Plans were made for accommodating an additional 3,000 children in reservation schools during the 1963-1964 school year; however the increase in children ready to enter school will also be 3,000. In the Intermountain School established in former Army hospital at Brigham City, Utah, there are facilities for 2,400 Navaho pupils. Others have been sent to California, Kansas, and other states. Taking the children so far from home has been hard on them and on their parents, but the Navaho are determined that their children shall have an education to prepare them for work in the outside world.

In 1957 the Navaho Tribal Council voted $200,000 to be used for scholarships for their young people, and now has a $10,000,000 trust fund from which the income shall provide future scholarship funds. These are particularly for young men and women who wish to train for professions. Each receives $1,200 per year, with $2,000 for married students, based on need, which is not paid back in money, but in service to the tribe.

The University of New Mexico has an Indian student organization, called the Kiva Club, which also raises scholarship money for new students through performances of Indian dance teams from many pueblos, and from non-Pueblo groups. These are given in the University gymnasium in Albuquerque, the use of which is donated to the Kiva Club without charge. Among those helped are Indian girls who will receive full training as registered nurses. Some will also attend the School for Practical Nurses at the Indian School, Albuquerque, which now graduates two classes annually of forty each.

The Kiva Club, due to the zeal of one of its members, John Olguin of Isleta – a political science major at the university – and an enthusiastic committee, has undertaken a program for summer recreation work in the pueblos of Isleta, Zia, and Jemez. This "Project Awareness II" has been granted $1,000 by the Student Senate to help launch this very worthwhile activity.

Scholarships for higher education are still a great need. The Southwestern Association on Indian Affairs has a fund for this purpose and solicits further contributions. It is constantly hearing of young Indians, well adapted for higher education, who must remain at housework or laborer's work because they cannot afford to prepare themselves for teaching or other professions.

The first Science Fair on the Navaho reservation was held in Gorman Hall at the fair grounds at Window Rock, 19-24 April 1963. Junior and senior high school students, the reservation over, participated; about 100 projects were submitted. Firms and civic groups in the area contributed $450 in awards and trophies. Thus stimulated, the Navaho Council anticipates affiliating with the Science Service in Washington, D. C.,

with the expectation of having Navaho students participating in the national competition by 1964.

The Pueblo Indians in New Mexico are learning slowly the power of their votes. At the election in February, the incumbent Indian member of the Jemez Springs School Board was re-elected, and another man from the pueblo was elected. Fortunately, a third member is friendly toward the Indians, which means that there is a majority on the school board eager to consider the educational needs of Indians in the public schools.

Also indicative of progress being made is the publication of newspapers by the Indians themselves. The Navaho initiated a paper, *The Navaho Times,* as a project of the Public Relations and Information department. Now in volume IV, it is published at Window Rock; subscription rate is $3.50 per year. Last year, the Jicarilla Apache launched a paper, *The Jicarilla Chieftain.* These and other publications issued by the various Indian groups serve as educational media not only for the Indians, but for the non-Indians as well. The Navaho have taken an active part in radio communications for a number of years.

Some may wonder as to its educational merit, but those who advocate the abolishment of the Bureau of Indian Affairs and termination of federal trusteeship of Indians, will see it as a step along the path toward that day when the indigenous peoples, like those who followed them to this continent, become a part of the whole citizenry of the United States of America. Again it is the Jicarilla who have set a historic precedent in New Mexico. Recently, the state liquor director approved a liquor license for the Apaches of that reservation. His action was approved by the Governor, the Bureau of Indian Affairs, and by the Jicarilla officials. It authorizes the first sale of liquor on Indian lands in the state. The action results from a change in federal law, made about ten years ago, which allows liquor on Indian reservations, subject to tribal restrictions and state law. It is the feeling of the Jicarilla that those who wish to drink liquor will do so. Up to the securing of this license, they had to purchase their drinks at off-reservation places. This could mean hazardous driving afterwards. Having the right of purchase in Dulce, the Jicarilla will be in their home surroundings; if policing is necessary, it will be close at hand.

Land Development and Power

With the construction of the Navaho dam on the San Juan river, at a cost of around $40 million, there is assurance that 110,000 acres of desert Indian land will be irrigated. The dam will also irrigate some non-Indian land in San Juan county, New Mexico, and bring additional water into the Rio Grande for irrigation and other purposes. Approval of this project was long opposed by Texas and California because they feared they would lose some of the water which now flows to them through the Colorado or Rio Grande rivers, and others opposed to it on the basis that the expense would not be justified through agricultural production or the development of hydroelectric power. From time to time, government economy drives and concentration on the missile race threatened the dam, but it was completed, and was duly dedicated in 1962. Some water filling has taken place behind the dam.

Last year, Congress authorized an expenditure of $140 million for the development of the irrigation project below the dam, in the area between Farmington and Gallup.

The potentials offered by the Navaho dam cannot be measured wholly in dollars and cents. The Navaho reservation cannot presently support one-half of its population, now in excess of 92,000, and increasing annually at a notable rate. Although many young Indians will be trained in the coming years to go into the non-Indian world, many are unhappy away from home, and population pressure is increasing outside as well as within the reservation. The additional irrigation from the Navaho dam, it is estimated, will support 10,000 people.

The Zuñi are also claiming irrigation water for 8,500 acres of Zuñi land, in a suit between Arizona and California, from the Colorado river. The federal government has introduced records to support these claims dating back as far as 1689, and it is probable that the Zuñi will win the suit.

Needless to say, the completion of the great Glen Canyon dam, on the Colorado river near the Utah-Arizona border, will affect the whole region and bring many changes to the Navaho and other Indians dwelling thereabouts. Already the modern city of Page, Arizona, has sprung into being, and other towns are envisaged. Scheduled for completeion early in 1964, the Glen Canyon dam will be 710 feet high and will make possible the filling of a large water body to be known as Lake Powell. The lakes created in the Navaho country will be highly developed recreation centers, with all their attendant business enterprises and employment opportunities.

The Jicarilla Apache have benefited by several million dollars in bonus money and rentals since oil and gas were discovered on their reservation in 1951, and they have developed their timber resources to the point where the annual income is notable. A large portion of the Jicarilla funds has been set aside for administration, herd improvement, health and welfare, and other programs designed to improve and develop their resources and to help raise the standards of living.

Although electric power has been available to the Rio Grande pueblos and many other Indian groups for a considerable time, electricity has just recently reached the Hopi. Today, 60 miles of power lines are strung across that remote reservation. The traditionalist fought unsuccessfully to prevent electrification of the villages; just the opposite results obtain at Taos, where time after time the progressives have failed in their attempt to get electricity into the pueblo. The same pertains to Taos sanitation; the traditionalists have voted down all efforts to introduce modern toilets and sewage disposal. During the past year, Arizona Public Service Company has extended its power lines to Hopiland so that electrical current is available to all villages. This, in addition to good roads has brought about an influx of tourists. The Hopi for the first time have become interested in the tourist trade and industrial development. Overnight accommodations are not adequate, but plans are in the formative stage to alleviate that deficiency.

Although the Taos Indians get their water from the stream that runs through their pueblo, they suffer no ill results. In one way at least, they are satisfactorily progressive: the doctor stationed at the pueblo reports that virtually all Taos babies are now delivered in the Public Health Service hospital at the pueblo. He says that "Last year we had 33 deliveries, and only one was a home delivery and that was an accident."

A valuable undertaking has been initiated at the pueblo of Picurís, where official permission was granted archaeologists from the Fort Burgwin Research Center, near Taos, to excavate in an ancient section of the village. The digging has gone through nearly 800 years of refuse accumulations. It is planned to uncover the ruins, restore the chambers involved, and turn them over to the Picurís people, who expect to profit from the visitors who come to the pueblo. They hope to develop a museum and other attractions. Already they offer guided tours for a modest fee.

The pueblo of San Juan, on whose lands the first Spanish settlers in New Mexico established themselves and the initial place of Christian worship as well as their first real seat of government, is likewise enjoying the benefits of archaeological investigations. Archaeologists of the Museum of New Mexico excavated there in 1945 and determined the site of the capital founded by Onate in 1598. In recent years, field sessions have been held there by the University of New Mexico, and additional rooms were uncovered. As a result, the Indians of San Juan have been interested in protecting the excavated area. It has been fenced, and an admission charge is made.

The Navaho, with current budget of $19,500,000 from reservation resources, are putting all of their income into improved conditions for the people and for further development of the Navaho.

The resources on Indian lands are very tempting to certain of the law makers; they desire to make legal the purchase and exploitation of Indian holdings by non-Indians.

State Commissions on Indian Affairs have been set up in New Mexico and Arizona to investigate state Indian problems and to promote a more sympathetic understanding of Indians.

Indian girl making silver jewelry in a shop in Santa Fe

Southwestern Association on Indian Affairs
Annual Indian Arts and Crafts Market and Dances

The Annual Indian Arts & Crafts Market takes place in Santa Fe on the third Saturday and Sunday of August in a block long area between the historic Palace of the Governors and the ancient Plaza where Indians have gathered since the founding of Santa Fe in 1609 and which marks the end of the famed Santa Fe Trail.

Beginning with the first "Indian Fair" in Santa Fe in 1923, the Association has sponsored an annual market for Indian arts and crafts at which prizes are awarded. The objective of the Association is the encouragement of excellence in production, the revival of traditional patterns and the creation of good contemporary design.

In advance of the Market, SWAIA sends letters to all Pueblo Governors and Tribal Officials in the area requesting their co-operation in notifying their people. Individual invitations, with rules and qualifications, together with a list of prizes being offered, are mailed directly to hundreds of artists and craftsmen living within traveling distance of Santa Fe.

By dawn on Market day the Indians are arriving to artistically arrange their wares on colorful blankets under the Portal of the Palace. To accommodate the ever increasing number of craftsmen competing each year, the Association provides additional "stalls" under rows of brilliant red, gold and turquoise canvas.

Cash awards are given in 20 categories. Judging is conducted in the early morning of the first day so the prize winners can display their ribbons on their work and naturally obtain a better price for those pieces. The judges, all specialists in Indian arts, are recruited by the Association from the staff of the Museum of New Mexico, Indian traders and well-known private collectors.

Indian dance groups perform in the Patio of the Palace twice each afternoon. A nominal admission charge is made to pay the dancers and to help defray some of the expenses of the Market for which there is no admission charge. One program of three or four dances is performed twice on Saturday and a different program is performed twice on Sunday. Only authentic dances are performed by adult dance groups wearing traditional costumes. A jury of all Indian judges awards a cash prize to the best dance group each day. This is a unique opportunity to see several ceremonial dances which are seldom performed or may be seen only by traveling to many Pueblos or Reservations at all seasons of the year.

The Annual Indian Market offers visitors and collectors a rare occasion to see and to choose from a great variety of the finest pottery and jewelry as well as a selection of paintings, textiles, baskets, rugs and drums, and to deal personally with the many artists and craftsmen so seldom gathered together.

Southwestern Association on Indian Affairs
Exhibit of Genuine & Imitation Indian Arts & Crafts

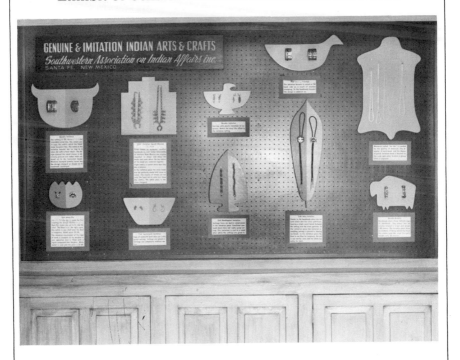

The above photograph shows one side of the exhibit of Genuine & Imitation Indian Arts & Crafts designed and constructed by the Association for display in the New Mexico State Pavilion of the New York World's Fair in 1964 and 1965. Following the Fair, the exhibit will be on permanent display in Santa Fe.

The showcase is 4' high and 8' long with glass enclosed display panels on both sides. The case is mounted on a handsome base cabinet of native pine with southwestern motif.

The articles include many examples of jewelry together with rugs and drums. The genuine article and its imitation counterpart are mounted in pairs, on forms of Indian design, above an interesting explanation of how the "true" differs from the "false".

The Association's objective in sponsoring this exhibit is to give the public an opportunity to appreciate and recognize this inimitable native art and to caution them against misrepresentation.

See page 101 for article *The Genuine and the Imitation in Indian Arts and Crafts.*

Calendar of Indian Ceremonies

NOTE: DO NOT TAKE PICTURES, MAKE SKETCHES OR TAKE NOTES WITHOUT FIRST OBTAINING PERMISSION. THIS IS VERY IMPORTANT.

January	1	Taos Turtle Dance (generally); dances in many of the pueblos on New Year's and three succeeding days.
	6	King's Day dances in most of the pueblos (installation of governors), including Buffalo or Deer Dance at Taos and Eagle Dance at San Ildefonso. Many of the pueblos have dances on the three succeeding days.
	23	San Ildefonso feast day, Animal Dance in one plaza, Comanche Dance in other.
February	2	San Felipe Buffalo Dance; also dances in several other pueblos.
	4-5	Llano Dances, Los Comanches, at Taos (Spanish-American interpretation of Plains dances).
	15	Dances at San Juan.
March-April		Easter Sunday and succeeding two or three days, dances in most of the pueblos; ceremonial foot races. Several of the pueblos observe ditch-opening ceremonies with dances, and some play ceremonial shinny.

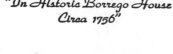

CALENDAR OF INDIAN CEREMONIES *(continued)*

March	27	Dances generally at the Keresan pueblos and Jemez
April		Last Saturday — Nizhoni Dances at the Johnson Gymnasium, University of New Mexico, Albuquerque.
May	1	San Felipe feast day, Corn Dance.
	3	Taos, Ceremonial Races, (c. 8:00-10:00 a.m.); Cochiti Corn Dance (Coming of the Rivermen).
	29-June 4	Tesuque, a dance during this week.
June	8	Santa Clara Buffalo Dance.
	13	Sandía feast day Corn Dance; observance of San Antonio's Day dances at Taos (Corn Dance), San Juan, Santa Clara, San Ildefonso, Cochiti, and Paguate.
	24	San Juan's Day dances at Taos (afternoon), San Juan, Isleta,* Cochiti, Santa Ana, Laguna, and Acoma; Jemez Rooster Pull.

*Since Isleta adopted its constitution, the ceremonial calendar has undergone various changes. One may see dances performed by either the Laguna group which dwells in the pueblo, or by the Isleta group. Dates should be checked annually.

June	29	San Pedro's Day at Laguna, Acoma, Santa Ana, San Felipe, Santo Domingo, Cochiti, and Isleta—Generally Rooster Pulls.
July	1-4	Mescalero Apache *Gahan* Ceremonial. Dances at the Indian Pow-Wow. Flagstaff.
	4	Jicarilla Apache Feast (no ceremonies).
	14	Cochiti feast day, Corn Dance.
	25-26	Taos Corn Dance.
	25	Santiago's Day at Santa Ana and Laguna; Acoma, Rooster Pull; Cochiti Corn Dance; Taos Corn Dance.
	26	Santa Ana's feast day; Santa Ana, Taos and Acoma Corn Dances.
August	2	Jemez, Old Pecos Bull Dance.
	4	Santo Domingo feast day, Corn Dance.
	10	Picuris feast day; San Lorenzo's Day at Laguna and Acomita, Corn Dances.
	12	Santa Clara, Corn Dance.
	15	Zia feast day, Corn Dance.
mid-August		Dances at the Inter-tribal Indian Ceremonial at Gallup, N. M., on the second Thurs., Fri., Sat., Sun., in August.
late-August		Dances in plaza of Governor's Palace in Santa Fe in conjunction with Annual Indian Market sponsored by Southwestern Association on Indian Affairs.

CALENDAR OF INDIAN CEREMONIES (continued)

late-August   Hopi Snake Dances (check locally)
             28 Isleta feast day.

September   2 Acoma feast day, Corn Dance.
             8 San Ildefonso, Harvest Dance.*

Sept.   14-15 Jicarilla Apache celebration at Horse or Stone Lake.
mid-Sept.   Navajo Fair, Window Rock, Arizona
          19 Laguna feast day, Harvest Dance and others.
          29 Taos, Sundown Dance.
          30 Taos feast day, relay races and pole climbing.

October   First week, annual Navajo Fair at Shiprock, N. M.
           4 Nambé feast day.
    31-Nov. 2 On one of these days, ceremonies in most of the pueblos.

*Because so many San Ildefonso Indians work at Los Alamos, the ceremonies traditionally held at this time of the year have been shifted to the weekend closest to the old dates. The same situation prevails at San Juan, Santa Clara, and Tesuque with regard to dances. Check dates annually.

November   1   *(see* Oct. 31).   Taos dance

            12   Jemez and Tesuque feast d

November-   Some time in November or December, the *Shalako* at Zuñi.
December   Navajo Night Way and Mountain Top Way ceremonies.

December   24   Taos, night procession and pine bonfires.
               Christmas Eve dances in mission churches at Acoma, La-
                  guna, Isleta, San Felipe, Santo Domingo, Tesuque, Taos,
                  and possibly others.

            25   Taos Deer or Matachines dances (afternoon).
               Christmas Day and two or three days following, dances at
                  most of the pueblos.

            31   *New Year's Eve,* Sandía Deer Dance.
               In the various Hopi villages, katsina (kachina) dances are
                  held from December-July. These may be seen frequently
                  on Saturday or Sunday.

Suggested Reading List

The Navajo and Pueblo Silversmiths . . . . John Adair
New Mexico . . . . American Guide Series
Book of Indians (narrative by Wm. Brandon) . . . . . American Heritage
Navaho Weavings: Its Technique and History   } . C. A. Amsden
Prehistoric Southwesterners from Basketmaker to Pueblo }
"The Pueblo Kachina cult," S. W. Journ. of Anthropology,
Vol. II (Winter, 1955) . . . . F. G. Anderson
In Navajo Land . . . . Laura Armer
Blood Brother . . . . Elliott Arnold
Savage Son . . . . Oren Arnold
* The Winged Serpent (an anthology) . . . . Margot Astrov
Navajos, Gods, and Tom-Toms . . . . A. H. Babington, M. D.
America's Buried Past . . . . Gordon C. Baldwin
The Delight Makers . . . . A. F. Bandelier
Beautyway, a Navaho Ceremony (1957) . . . . Bollingen Series
Pima and Papago Indian Agriculture . . . E. F. Castetter and W. H. Bell
The Pottery of Santo Domingo Pueblo } . . . . K. M. Chapman
Pueblo Pottery (portfolios) }
The Hopi-Tewa of Arizona, Univ. of Calif. Pub. in Am. Arch.
and Ethn., (1954), Vol. 44 No. 3: 259-376 . . . . Edward P. Dozier

* The titles shown with asterisk are available in paper back editions

Note - A few of the titles are out-of-print but copies may still be obtained through the book stores advertised herein.

READING LIST (continued)

Comparative Studies of North American
Indians (1957). . . . . H. E. Driver and W. C. Massey
"America's First Painters," *The National Geographic*
Magazine (March, 1955). Dorothy Dunn
* *Friendly People: the Zuñi Indians* (1963) ⎫
* *Let's Explore Indian villages past and present* (1962) ⎬ . B. P. Dutton
* *Navaho Weaving Today* (1962) ⎭
Social Organization of the Western Pueblos . . . . Fred Eggan
"Authoritative Control and the Society System ⎫
in Jemez Pueblo," *S. W. Journ. of Anthro.,* ⎪
Vol. 9, No. 4 (1953) , Albuquerque ⎪
"Jemez Kiva Magic and Its Relation to Features ⎪
of Prehistoric Kivas," *S. W. Journ of Anthro.,* ⎬ . . . Florence H. Ellis
Vol. 8, No. 2 (1952), Albuquerque ⎪
"Patterns of Aggression and the War Cult in ⎪
Southwestern Pueblos," *S. W. Journ. of Anthro.,* ⎪
Vol. 7, No. 2 (1951), Albuquerque ⎭
American Indian Dance Steps . . . . Bessie and May G. Evans
* "Indian Baskets," Texas Memorial Museum,
Austin (1952) . . . . Glen T. Evans and T. N. Campbell
"The Line-break, problem child of Pueblo pottery"
El Palacio, vol. 58, No. 9 (1951), Santa Fe. . . . . . . K. M. Chapman
and Bruce Ellis
* *Indians of the Americas*
* *On the Gleaming Way* . . . . John Collier
Black Sand: prehistory in North America ⎫
Hopi Kachina Dolls ⎬ . . . . H. S. Colton
Zuñi Folk Tales . . . . F. H. Cushing
The Indians of the Southwest, Okla. Press (1951). . . . . E. E. Dale
"Music of Santo Domingo Pueblo, New Mexico" ⎫
S. W. Museum Papers No. 3, Los Angeles ⎬
"Music of Acoma, Isleta, Cochiti, and Zuñi Pueblos," ⎬ Frances Densmore
Bureau of American Ethnology, Bull. 165 (1957) ⎭
The Sobaipuri Indians of the upper San ⎫
Pedro river valley, southeastern Arizona ⎪
The upper Pima of San Cayetano del Tuma- ⎬ . . . . C. C. Di Peso
cacori: an archaeohistorical recon- ⎪
struction of the Ootam of Pimeria Alta ⎭
Indian Art in America ⎫
Kachinas and the White Man ⎬ . . . . F. J. Dockstader
"Factionalism at Taos Pueblo, New Mexico," *Anthro. Papers,*
Bureau of American Ethnology (1957) . . . . William N. Fenton
Indians and Other Americans: two ways of
life meet . . . . H. E. Fey and D. McNickle
The Snake Dance of the Hopi Indians (1961) . . . . E. R. Forrest

READING LIST (continued)

The Pueblos: a camera chronicle ⎫
The Rio Grande: river of destiny ⎭ . . . . Laura Gilpin
Isleta Paintings (Introd. and commentary by
E. C. Parsons), *Bull.* 181, Bur. of Amer.
Ethnology (1962) . . . . E. S. Goldfrank (Ed.)
Pueblo Pottery Making (San Ildefonso) . . . . C. E. Guthe
Head and Face Masks in Navaho Ceremonialism ⎫
Star Lore among the Navaho ⎭ . . . . . Berard Haile
Emergence Myth (Navaho) . . . Berard Haile and M. C. Wheelwright
Paint the Wind ⎫
Spin a Silver Dollar ⎭ . . . . Alberta Hannum
Pajarito Plateau and Its Ancient People ⎫
The Pueblo Indian World ⎭ E. L. Hewett and B. P. Dutton
Landmarks of New Mexico . . . . E. L. Hewett and W. L. Mauzy
"Prehistoric paintings at Pottery Mound,"
Archaeology, Vol. 13, no. 4 (1960) . . . . F. C. Hibben
The Kachinas Are Coming . . . . Gene M. Hodge
People of the Blue Water (Walapai and Havasupai Indians)
(1954) Harper Bros., N. Y. . . . . Flora G. Iliff
Indian Life (magazine of the Inter-tribal Indian Ceremonial, Gallup, N.M.)
Indian News (newsletter of the N.M. Commission on Indian Affairs,
Santa Fe)

READING LIST (continued)

Redman, Whiteman . . . . H. C. James
"The Western Apache Clan System: its origins and development," Univ. of N. M. Pubs. in Anthro. No 9 (1957) . . Charles R. Kaut
"Indians of the Southwest," first annual report, Bureau
of Ethnic Research, Univ, of Ariz., Tucson, 1953 . . . . . Wm. H. Kelly
"Indian Affairs and the Indian Reorganization Act:
the 20 Year Record," Papers from 52d Amer. Anthro.
Assn. Symposium, Univ. of Ariz., Tucson, 1954 . . Wm. H. Kelly (Ed.)
The Story of Navaho Weaving (1961) . . . . Kate P. Kent
Where the Two Came to Their Father (text and portfolio) . . . Jeff King
Navaho Witchcraft . . . . C. Kluckhohn
* The Navaho . . . . C. Kluckhohn and D. C. Leighton
Pictorial History of the American Indian ⎫
The Changing Indian   ⎬ . . . . Oliver La Farge
                                         ⎭
The Navajo Door . . . . A. H. and D. C. Leighton
Cochiti, Univ. of Texas Press, Austin (1959) . . . . Lange
Seeking Life, Memoirs, Am. Folklore Soc., Vol. 50 (1959) . . Vera Laskie
Children of the People (Navaho) . . . D. C. Leighton and C. Kluckhohn
Navaho Means People . . . . Leonard McCombe, E. Z. Vogt
                                                       and C. Kluckhohn
Indian Traders
Richard Wetherill, Anasazi . . . . Frank McNitt
* Greener Fields: experiences among the American Indians ⎫
Indians of the Four Corners   ⎬ . . . . Alice
María: the Potter of San Ildefonso   ⎬   Marriott
* These Are the People   ⎭
"Aboriginal American Basketry," Report of
the U. S. National Museum (1904) . . . . O. T. Mason
"The Mountain Chant, a Navajo Ceremony," ⎫
5th annual report, Bureau of American   ⎪
Ethnology (1887), Washington   ⎬ . Washington Matthews
"Navaho Night Chant," Anthro. Ser., Vol. 5, ⎪
American Museum of Natural History,   ⎪
New York   ⎭
* Indian Silverwork of the Southwest   ⎫
Navaho Textile Arts   ⎪
The "Rain Bird" – A Study in Pueblo Design ⎬ . . . . H. P. Mera
Pueblo Indian Embroidery   ⎪
Style Trends of Pueblo Pottery   ⎭
"Hopi Agriculture and Food,"   ⎫
Reprint Series No. 5 (1954), Flagstaff   ⎪
"Hopi Customs, Folklore, and Ceremonies," ⎬ . . . . Museum of
Reprint Series No. 4 (1954), Flagstaff   ⎪   Northern Arizona
"Hopi History," Reprint Series No. 2   ⎪
(1951), Flagstaff   ⎭

READING LIST (continued)

"Hopi Indian Arts and Crafts,"
Reprint Series No. 3 (1951), Flagstaff
"Navajo Customs: Ethnographic Notes,'
Reprint Series No. 6 (1954), Flagstaff
} Museum of Northern Arizona

"Navaho 'Channel' Turquoise and Silver,"
El Palacio, Vol. 61, No. 12 (1954), Santa Fe . . . . . . David Neumann
Navajo Omens and Taboos . . . . Franc J. Newcomb
Sandpainting of the Navajo Shooting Chant . . . . . .Franc J. Newcomb
and Gladys Reichard

"Childhood and youth in Jicarilla Apache,"
Hodge Anniversary Pub. Fund, Vol. 4-5
"Myths and tales of the Jicarilla Apache
Indians,"
} . . . . M. E. Opler

Pueblo Indian Religion (2 vols.) . . . . Elsie C. Parsons
† *The Tewa Indian of the Hopi Country,* PLATEAU, V.25
No. 1, July 11, 1952 . . . . Erik K. Reed
Navajo Religion (2 vols.)
Navaho Shepherd and Weaver
Spider Woman: a story of Navajo weavers
} . . . . . Gladys A. Reichard

The Utes, a forgotten people . . . . Wilson Rockwell

† PLATEAU, a quarterly published by Northern Arizona Society of Science and Art, Inc. (Flagstaff), contains many articles on the Indians of Arizona.

* *Ceremonial Costumes of the Pueblo Indians* . . . Virginia M. Roediger
Apache Land . . . . .Ross Santee
Fruitland, N. Mexico, (a Navajo community in transition)
Cornell U. Press (1960) . . . . Tom T. Sasaki
* *Rock Art in the Navajo Reservoir District* . . . . . . .Polly Schaafsma
* *Decorative Art of the Southwestern Indians* . . . . . Dorothy Smith Sides
"American Indians and Indian Life," *Annals,* Amer.
Academy of Political and Social Sci., Vol. 311 (1957),
Cambridge . . . . (Eds.) George E. Simpson and J. M. Yinger
"Kiva Mural Decorations at Awatovi and Kawaika-a,"
Papers, Vol. XXXVII, *Peabody Mus. of Amer.*
Arch. and Ethn., Harvard Univ. (1952), Cambridge . . . .Watson Smith
The Mescalero Apaches, Univ. of Okla. Press (1958) . C. L. Sonnichsen
Cycles of Conquest (1961) . . . . E. H. Spicer
"The Zuñi Indians" (masks, Shalako ceremony etc.),
23rd anl. rept., *Bureau of Amer. Ethnology* (1904),
Washington . . . . M. C. Stevenson
Bird's-Eye View of the Pueblos . . . . .Stanley A. Stubbs
Southwest Indian Painting . . . . Clara Lee Tanner
Culture in Crisis: a study of the Hopi Indians. . . . . . Laura Thompson
First Penthouse Dwellers of America (revised)
"Here Comes the Navajo,"
U. S. Indian Service (1953)
The Papago Indians of Arizona and their relatives the Pima,
Sherman phamphlets No. 3 (1940), Haskel Inst.   Ruth M.
Lawrence, Kan. . . . .   Underhill
"Pueblo Crafts," *U. S. Indian Service,*
Education Division (1945)
"Work a Day Life of the Pueblos," *U. S. Indian Service,*
Education Division (1946)
Old Father, the story teller, (1960) Dale Stewart King . . Pablita Velarde
Sitting Bull . . . . Stanley Vestal
Masked Gods (Navaho and Pueblo ceremonialism)
* *The Man Who Killed the Deer*   . . . Frank Waters
A Pima Remembers (1959) . . . . George Webb
Hail Chant and Water Chant
Navajo Creation Myth   . . . . Mary C. Wheelwright
Myth and Prayer of the Great Star Chant and the Myth of the
Coyote Clan . . . . Mary C. Wheelwright and D. P. McAllester
The Pueblo of Sia, New Mexico, Bull. 184,
Bur. of Amer. Ethnology (1962) . . . . L. A. White
* *Ancient Man in North America,* 4th ed., (revised),
Popular Series No. 4, Colo.
Mus. of Natural History, Denver . . . . H. M. Wormington

READING LIST (continued)

* *Prehistoric Indians of the Southwest* (on modern Indians also),
Popular Series No. 7, Colo. Mus. of Natural
History, Denver . . . . H. M. Wormington
"Sandpaintings of the Kayenta Navaho,"
Univ. of N. M. Pubs. in Anthro. No. 7 (1952) . . . Leland C. Wyman
"The Navajo Year Book of Planning in Action," (1955), Window Rock
"The Navajo Yearbook," (1961), Window Rock . . . . . Robert W. Young
"The Ramah Navajo" (1949)
"The Trouble at Round Rock" (1952) } . . . Robert W. Young and
"Selections from Navajo History" (1953) William Morgan
This is a Hopi Kachina, Museum of Northern Arizona
(1962) . . . . Barton Wright and Evelyn Roat

Many of the works here listed contain bibliographies.

159

Zuñi Shalako ceremony personator, painting by Awa Tsireh.